200 Quick and Simple Recipes to
Lose the Weight, and Find Your Pat

WHEAT BELLY

30-MINUTE (OR LESS!) COOKBOOK

WILLIAM DAVIS, MD

Collins

Published by Collins, an imprint of HarperCollins Publishers Ltd,
by arrangement with Rodale Inc.

First Canadian edition

HarperCollins Publishers Ltd
2 Bloor Street East, 20th Floor
Toronto, Ontario, Canada
M4W 1A8

www.harpercollins.ca

Photographs by Linda Pugliese • Food styling by Carrie Ann Purcell • Prop styling by Molly FitzSimons
Book design by Carol Angstadt and Amy King

Library and Archives Canada Cataloguing in Publication information is available upon request.

ISBN 978-1-44342-486-8

Printed and bound in the United States
RRD 9 8 7 6 5 4 3 2 1

Dedicated to the
followers of *Wheat Belly,*
who asked for something
quick and easy!

CONTENTS

INTRODUCTION

The Wheat-Free Lifestyle in 30 Minutes (or Less!)

WHAT CAN YOU accomplish in 30 minutes or less? In today's electronically connected world, you could publish a few comments on Facebook or post a few Tweets. Or you could walk on your treadmill for a little exercise, vacuum a couple of rooms, or read another chapter in a novel. You could light some candles, darken the lights, grab your spouse . . . okay, enough of that!

Or you could take action that helps you and your family make a huge leap toward better health and prepare a meal that frees all of you from the appetite-stimulating, health-impairing, visceral fat–accumulating effects of modern wheat, enjoying quick and delicious meals that satisfy everyone weaned from the breast on up!

Since the original *Wheat Belly* was published in August 2011, followed by the *Wheat Belly Cookbook,* an international movement has been launched, a dietary revolution now embraced by millions of people eager to regain control over appetite, weight, and health. We certainly cannot credit my charm, wit, or good looks—it's the *power of the message* and the wonderful stories of success that pour in day after day, month after month, that have catapulted this message into the spotlight.

We've witnessed what happens to people who take the brave leap and do the *opposite* of what conventional advice tells us: Weight and health are *transformed.* A long list of health conditions diminish or disappear. Most typically, people experience relief from acid reflux, bowel urgency, joint pain, and mental "fog." Many diabetics become *non*diabetic. People suffering for years with the pain and deformity of inflammatory and autoimmune conditions experience markedly reduced symptoms, or even outright cure. Depression lifts in many, while anxiety and paranoia disappear in others. The food obsessions of bulimia and binge eating disorder can dissipate within days. And, of course, pounds of fat, mostly from the inflammatory visceral fat of the abdomen, the infamous "wheat belly," shrink sufficiently to allow you to dust off the "skinny jeans" you saved in the back of the closet or comfortably wear the several-sizes-smaller dress or trousers from 20 years earlier.

We choose to liberate ourselves from all things wheat, while also rejecting the processed gluten-free foods made with junk carbohydrate ingredients (cornstarch, rice starch/flour, potato starch, tapioca starch), as well as processed foods (which nearly *all* contain wheat).

Though we can relearn many important dietary lessons by simply recalling many of the habits of our grandparents or great grandparents, most of us have no desire to return to the 2, 3, 4, or more hours of preparation that were often required to prepare a full meal in their day. Thus, the quick, 30-minute or less, wheat-free effort you're now holding in your hands.

"Giving Up Wheat and Junk Carbs Is Too Hard!"

Or I might hear that it is too time-consuming, or too inconvenient, or involves too many hard-to-find ingredients.

No question: There is a period of adjustment required. After all, we creatures of the early 21st century have allowed, both purposely and inadvertently, modern wheat to balloon to 20 percent of all the calories we eat. For some people, it can be as high as 50 percent of calories, given the convenience, portability, ubiquity, and *addictive properties* of this creation of genetics research called "wheat." Banning it from your diet and that of your family means an abrupt break from long-standing habits. It means no longer relying on frozen dinners and delivery pizza. It means breakfast, lunch, and dinner—at least at first—need to be rethought, planned out until new habits are established, with the right mix of ingredients stocked in your pantry and refrigerator, and even new sources located to purchase ingredients. There is indeed an up-front investment in time and effort.

But neither do you want to devote all of your time to making this conversion.

This was the motivation for the *Wheat Belly 30-Minute (or Less!) Cookbook*, a collection of tools and ideas to help you compress the time required to navigate this new enlightened lifestyle. While we lack the convenience (with all the health compromises) of microwaving a frozen dinner in 3 minutes, or the grab-and-run appeal of a Pop-Tart, we can adopt a number of important methods to reduce the time commitment required to adhere to this unique but enormously effective approach.

To conform to such a tight timeline, I've employed several easy, commonsense, time-saving strategies, such as having a premade supply of the All-Purpose Baking Mix (page 19) on hand, a blend of healthy ingredients sans wheat and junk carbohydrates that can be used to create muffins, rolls, or focaccia flatbread ahead of time (on the weekend, for example), which are then stored in the refrigerator for use over the course of the week. (Healthy wheat-free products are just starting to become a commercial reality but are not yet available to most people.) You will find a wide variety of sauces, dressings, and dips that can convert a simple salmon fillet, for instance, into a delicious and exotic dish with just a dash of healthy sauce created with no unhealthy ingredients. There are wheat-free compliant seasoning mixes, too—with no junk fillers, such as wheat flour, cornstarch, or maltodextrin—that allow you to whip up delicious, fragrant, and spicy dishes with minimal effort while slashing several minutes off preparation time.

I also wander out of the 30-minute time constraint with several adventurous themed menus that collect several recipes into special occasions, such as Pub Night, Romantic Evening, and New Orleans Jamboree.

The goal: to allow you and your family to enjoy all the variety, flavor, and health benefits of wheatlessness without sacrificing the conveniences of modern lifestyles.

Some people are concerned that their new wheat-free diet will be more costly, as we lose the commoditized (and government-subsidized) cost advantages of modern wheat. But remember: We wheat-free folk consume 400 fewer calories per person, per day, meaning less food needs to be prepared or purchased, providing a considerable built-in advantage. A family of four can be expected to consume something like 1,600 fewer calories per day, approaching the daily caloric intake of another person. Most people following the wheat-free lifestyle who are in the habit of maintaining a grocery budget therefore report that overall food costs are either *unchanged* or modestly *lower* with the switch to wheatlessness.

If you are already a seasoned wheat-free adherent, then this new 30-minute (or less!) cookbook will add some new and easy possibilities for day-to-day meal preparation, as well as some unique ideas for special occasions. If you have come to believe that a life without wheat and other unhealthy foods has to be dull and tasteless, well, you've got some interesting, spicy, and delicious surprises coming your way! You will discover re-created ethnic foods, including Moroccan, Indian, Chinese, Mexican, and Italian dishes, as well as reimagined traditional American foods recast into this new wheat-free lifestyle. Pizzas, soups, sandwiches, muffins, cheesecake, barbecued pork—there are very few dishes that cannot be re-created minus all unhealthy ingredients in the 30-minute (or less!) timeline. And be sure to peruse the Snacks and Desserts section, as I believe you will encounter some delightful surprises!

For those of you new to this lifestyle, the recipes and meals featured here can help you get off to a confident and tasty start without overwhelming you in complexity or underwhelming you in taste. Yes, it will mean losing some old ingredients and gaining some new, plus a few new lessons to learn in baking, thickening, and ingredient choice. But reinvigorated health, potentially minus several health conditions, as well as several inches off your waist without the pull of appetite are your reward for your effort.

All right, let's get started. In the first chapter, I will discuss how several conveniences will be used in your wheat-free lifestyle to compress preparation time down to the desired 30-minute (or less!) timeline.

PUTTING TOGETHER YOUR WHEAT-FREE KITCHEN

START YOUR NEW wheat-free adventure by purging your shelves of all wheat and wheat-containing products. This is necessary to reduce the temptation to eat those chocolate-covered pretzels you've been saving and other goodies that can—even as the tiniest morsel—undo *everything* you've accomplished. It also minimizes the potential for future reexposures that can result in anything from gastrointestinal distress (bloating, cramps, diarrhea) to joint pain, asthma, and even emotional effects.

Next, you will need to do some shopping for wheat-free replacement ingredients. Your wheat-free life, for instance, will require some new flours to allow you to create sandwiches, cookies, and other baked goods using healthy nonwheat ingredients. And, for efficiency, especially to create dishes in a 30-minute timeline, a few new kitchen tools will be helpful. All in all, converting your kitchen to one that dispenses wonderfully healthy, tasty, and quick wheat-free dishes really just requires some adjustments to your previous wheat-filled life.

This book serves as a guide for everyone who wishes to eliminate wheat and gluten from their lives. Wheat elimination is *not* just for the celiac sufferer or the gluten-sensitive; it's for *everyone*. However, the advice and recipes here are indeed appropriate for the celiac sufferer and gluten-sensitive, though additional efforts will need to be made to accomplish meticulous gluten avoidance, especially looking for "gluten-free" on the label to avoid potential for cross-contamination.

But, before I get started on what you need to conduct your new life of wheatlessness, you first should . . .

Clean Your Kitchen!

Remember: Wheat products contain gliadin, which degrades in the gastrointestinal tract to a collection of opiates that bind to the opiate receptors of the brain. They don't cause euphoria or pain relief; they trigger appetite. Freeing yourself from the relentless appetite-stimulating effects of wheat, the frequent and intrusive thoughts of food, and the increased but unnecessary calorie intake all add up to a powerful way to control impulse, weight, and health.

Start by clearing your pantry of obvious wheat sources, such as bread, muffins, bagels, pitas, rolls, cookies, energy bars, and pastries. Don't forget the bag of wheat flour too: You will *never* need it.

After clearing the obvious wheat sources, clear the not-so-obvious sources. Examine the labels of *all* processed foods to see whether wheat in any form is found on the list of ingredients. See "Wheat . . . by Any Other Name!" on page 13 for a list of hidden sources of wheat—yes, it's long!

Common processed foods that contain wheat include:

- Bread crumbs, panko
- Breakfast cereals
- Canned soups
- Cookies
- Crackers
- Frozen dinners
- Frozen waffles and pancakes
- Granola bars
- Ice cream, frozen yogurt (cookie dough, cookies and cream)
- Instant soup mixes
- Macaroni and cheese mix
- Pancake mix
- Pastas
- Powdered soup mixes
- Pretzels
- Salad dressings—bottled and dry mixes
- Sauce mixes
- Sausages, processed meats

- Seasoning mixes
- Soy sauce, teriyaki sauce
- Twizzlers and other candies

Get rid of it all! Remember: The gliadin protein of wheat is powerfully addictive and will pull you back into its clutches. Don't let that happen!

Restocking the Shelves with Healthy Wheat-Free Foods

Once you've banished all wheat-containing foods from your kitchen, it will be time to restock with healthy replacements. Here are some basic ground rules to follow.

- Read labels. Look for "wheat," "wheat flour," "gluten," "vital wheat gluten," "modified food starch," "caramel coloring," or any of the other dozens of buzzwords for concealed wheat that manufacturers slip in. Refer to "Wheat . . . by Any Other Name!" on page 13 if you're unsure about a product. People with celiac disease and gluten sensitivity definitely need to do this, but this is also a good practice for everyone to minimize exposure, and especially to avoid the gastrointestinal and appetite-stimulating effects of wheat.

- Buy *single-ingredient natural foods* found in the produce aisle, from the butcher, and at farmers' markets that don't require labels. There are no labels, for instance, on tomatoes, portobello mushrooms, avocados, eggs, or salmon.

- Avoid processed foods with multiple ingredients. A salad dressing you make yourself with olive oil, vinegar, and herbs is far safer than a premixed bottled dressing with 15 ingredients.

- Lose the breakfast cereal habit. There is no such thing as a healthy breakfast cereal (at least not yet). They are land mines for wheat, not to mention other junk ingredients such as corn, sugar, high-fructose corn syrup, and additives.

- Never buy a processed or prepared food unless you can view the ingredient list. Processed meats at the deli, for instance, are frequent sources of unexpected wheat exposure. Ask to see the label. If you cannot, pass it by.

- Don't even bother with the bread aisle or bakery. There's *nothing* there you need!

- Avoid prepared foods made from ground meats, such as meatballs and meat loaf, as these nearly always contain bread crumbs.

- Ignore all claims of "heart healthy," "low fat," "low in cholesterol," "part of a balanced diet," etc. These claims are there for one reason: to persuade shoppers that an unhealthy food might have some health benefit. Rarely is that true. In fact, most "heart-healthy" foods *cause* heart disease!

- Get to know your grocery stores, farmers' markets, health food stores, and anyone else selling foods in your area. To make healthy wheat-free foods, you may need some ingredients that are not sold at all mainstream outlets. Prices also vary widely, so it helps to shop around and not be stuck with high prices for your everyday wheat-free ingredients.

Most of us who are trying to avoid wheat but are not among the most gluten-sensitive just need to look for foods and ingredients that do not list wheat or wheat-derived ingredients, while anyone with celiac disease or extreme gluten sensitivity will require an explicit "gluten-free" designation on the label. For instance, with dark chocolate chips, the most gluten-sensitive people will need to purchase a brand actually designated "gluten-free," meaning it contains no wheat and no gluten and has no potential for cross-contamination from other foods and facilities. Those of us avoiding wheat but without celiac disease or extreme gluten sensitivity can do fine with brands that are not labeled "gluten-free" but do not list any wheat or gluten equivalents in the ingredients.

Alternative Flours

When we remove wheat, we remove the primary staple for creating breads and other baked foods. We therefore require alternative meals and flours to recreate baked goods, but we must choose them carefully to avoid adding other problem ingredients. Recall that we also reject the typical replacement flours used in the gluten-free world: cornstarch, rice starch/flour, potato starch, and tapioca starch, due to their extravagant capacity to send blood sugar levels through the roof.

The flours and meals that we choose must be:

- Wheat-free

- Gluten-free if celiac disease or gluten sensitivity is present

- Free of conventional gluten-free junk carbohydrate ingredients—no cornstarch, potato starch, tapioca starch, or rice starch/flour

- Low in carbohydrate exposure; otherwise, we'll have high blood sugar levels and other undesirable phenomena. The dried, pulverized starch in flours can be especially destructive because the fine consistency increases surface area for digestion exponentially, resulting in rapid breakdown to blood sugar. So we need to strictly limit our exposure to carbohydrates in powdered form. The more good fats, protein, and fiber, the better!

- Otherwise healthy; we don't, therefore, replace a problem—wheat—with another problem

Our choices of meals and flours include:

Almond meal and flour	Pecan meal
Chia meal and flour	Psyllium seeds, ground
Coconut flour	Pumpkin seed meal
Garbanzo bean (chickpea) flour	Sesame seed meal
Ground golden flaxseeds	Sunflower seed meal
Hazelnut meal	Walnut meal

Note: As commonly used, "meal" refers to the end product of grinding *whole* nuts, including skins; "flour" refers to the end product of grinding *blanched* nuts with their skins removed, and sometimes with oils pressed out, yielding a finer flour texture and finer end result with baking.

(continued on page 8)

Important Reminders for the Gluten-Sensitive

People with celiac disease or equivalents, such as neurological impairment or dermatitis herpetiformis, and those with gluten sensitivity need to be meticulous in avoiding wheat, gluten, and nonwheat gluten sources such as barley, rye, triticale, bulgur, and oats. (Not all gluten-sensitive people have gluten reactions to the avenin protein in oats, but oatmeal and oat bran skyrocket your blood sugar anyway. So kiss it goodbye and you'll be better off. You will also avoid the common cross-contamination problems of oats, which are typically prepared in facilities that handle wheat products.) Not only is meticulous gluten avoidance necessary to avoid such things as violent bowel reactions, but it is important to avoid the manyfold higher risk of gastrointestinal cancers and progressive neurological impairment that comes from even occasional exposure.

So, unlike most of us non-gluten-sensitive folk who may experience "only" a bout of diarrhea, mental "fog" and fatigue, or hand pain for several days, genuinely gluten-sensitive people can experience dire long-term consequences and should make every possible effort to avoid exposures, purposeful or inadvertent.

Here are some important strategies to keep in mind above and beyond just avoiding wheat and gluten.

- Getting *everyone* in the house to give up wheat and gluten really helps make life easier. It reduces exposure to tempting foods, and it reduces the potential for contamination. Don't forget that your dog, cat, or other pet should also be consuming wheat- and gluten-free foods; dishing out their food is otherwise a potential exposure.

- If getting everyone else in the house to give up wheat and gluten is not possible, a diplomatic but firm segregation of foods, utensils, and cooking surfaces will be necessary. (The most extreme gluten-sensitive individuals cannot tolerate this compromise, however.) Separate pots and pans, serving tools, even plates, glasses, and utensils are necessary for many people.

- Help educate others that being wheat- and gluten-free is not just some food neurosis. It is how you manage *a disease condition,* just as someone with cancer requires chemotherapy. *Never* feel guilty about having to inform others about your needs.

- In a household in which there is segregation of foods and utensils, label foods so that you know which container of hummus, for instance, has had wheat-containing pita chips dipped into it. All it takes is someone dipping a knife into a jar of peanut butter after first buttering a slice of bread with it. Suddenly, the peanut butter that you thought was confidently gluten-free has now been contaminated and could trigger a disaster. Avoid sharing foods such as butter, nut butters, preserves, cream cheese, dips, and spreads, since the knife or food that contacts them may be contaminated.

- Eating outside the home is especially hazardous. Thankfully, some of the more progressive restaurants truly understand the concept of gluten cross-contamination, a trend that will spread, given the rapidly growing interest in eating wheat- and gluten-free. A meal at a restaurant where they forget and cook your food in a pan previously used to sauté breaded tilapia is all it takes to go down the wheat reexposure path. Adhere to this simple rule: If in doubt, don't.

- If you choose to take your chances at a restaurant, be especially careful to avoid breaded meats, foods fried in oils also used to fry bread crumb–coated foods or other wheat-containing foods, gravies, salad dressings, and most desserts. The most extremely gluten-sensitive, however, should not take even these risks.

- Check the label or check with the manufacturer of every prescription drug or nutritional supplement you take and make sure it is gluten-free.

- With rare exceptions, avoid fast-food restaurants. Sure, the salad may be gluten free and the salad dressing, too, but cross-contamination from buns and cookies prepared just a few feet away, or from using incompletely cleansed equipment, is all it takes to invite an exposure. Cross-contamination is the hurdle that many restaurants, fast-food and otherwise, have struggled with and the reason why many are reluctant to declare any of their dishes gluten-free.

- Be aware that gluten exposure can come via vehicles besides foods, including drugs, nutritional supplements, lipstick, chewing gum, shampoos, creams, and cosmetics. Wheat-containing shampoo, for instance, can often be the explanation for a persistent rash. If in doubt, check with the manufacturer, but don't be surprised if the answer you get is the usual corporate-speak and/or a disclaimer that they cannot guarantee something is gluten-free because of potential cross-contamination.

- Cross-contamination can occur even in single-ingredient foods during preparation, packaging, or display, such as bulk bins at the grocery store, a salad bar or food bar, or slicing meat with the same knife used to cut a sandwich.

All foods and ingredients in your kitchen, from refrigerator to pantry, should be gluten-free also, meaning not containing wheat or gluten sources—such as barley, rye, bulgur, triticale, and oats—and prepared in facilities that do not handle wheat or gluten products, so there is no potential for cross-contamination. These products will have "gluten-free" posted prominently on the package. But please, please, please remember: Many gluten-free foods are just junk carbohydrates in disguise, so be selective.

Let's face it: We live in a world dominated by this thing called wheat. Inadvertent exposures *will* occur. You can only do your best to keep exposures to an absolute minimum.

The following nonwheat meals and flours are excluded.

Rye, barley, oats, triticale, and bulgur are avoided due to immune cross-reactivity with wheat gluten.

Amaranth, teff, millet, chestnut, buckwheat, and quinoa are off the list because of excessive carbohydrate exposure (except when limiting carbohydrate exposure may not be as important, as in snacks or desserts for kids).

Cornstarch, rice starch/flour, potato starch, and tapioca starch—the typical gluten-free flours—are also off-limits, as mentioned earlier.

All flours should be stored in the refrigerator or freezer in an airtight container to slow oxidation. Alternatively, buy your nuts and seeds whole and grind them as you need them. A food processor, a high-quality food chopper (my little KitchenAid food chopper is worth its weight in gold!), or a coffee grinder all work, grinding a batch of whole nuts or seeds down to a meal or flour within 30 to 60 seconds. Grind only to a meal or flour consistency, as grinding further will yield nut or seed butters.

Combine flours to modify the texture of the eventual end product. For instance, in the All-Purpose Baking Mix (page 19), the primary flour is almond meal/flour, but with added coconut flour, ground golden flaxseeds, and a bit of psyllium seed—a combination that works better for most purposes than almond meal/flour alone.

Anyone with allergies to nut meals can find several potential replacement flour sources in this list, such as coconut flour and seed flours. However, note that, if you substitute, say, coconut and sesame seed flour for almond meal/flour in a recipe, some adjustment of liquid quantity and cooking time may be required.

Friendly Oils

Corollary to our rejection of the "healthy whole grain" message is our dismissal of the need to limit total fat, saturated fat, and cholesterol. In fact, we *add* fats and oils to our foods for their health benefits. Oils that were previously thought to be unhealthy, such as coconut oil due to saturated fat content, now make a return in this healthy, wheat-free lifestyle. Among the best oils to choose are:

- Avocado oil
- Coconut oil
- Extra-light olive oil
- Extra-virgin olive oil

- Flaxseed oil
- Organic butter and ghee
- Walnut oil

We also don't trim the fat off of our poultry, beef, pork, or fish and don't skim the gelatin and fat off our soup or stock. Lard is perfectly consistent with this lifestyle, but is tough to find in a nonhydrogenated form.

Sweeteners: What You Need to Know

There are several non- or minimally nutritive sweeteners that have proven to be relatively benign and are compatible with the *Wheat Belly 30-Minute (or Less!) Cookbook* program: stevia, erythritol, xylitol, luo han guo (monk fruit), and sucralose. These sweeteners allow you to re-create cookies, muffins, and other goodies without the adverse health effects of sugar, nor the unhealthy implications of some not-so-benign sweeteners, such as aspartame.

The sugar alcohols outside of erythritol and xylitol—such as mannitol, sorbitol, and maltitol—generate substantial gas, cramps, and diarrhea, not to mention increased blood sugar, and are therefore not recommended since most of us don't relish the prospect of diarrhea with dessert.

Combining sweeteners is an especially useful strategy. If, for example, you are among those who experience the bitter aftertaste of stevia, combine stevia with, say, erythritol or luo han guo; less stevia will be required and the aftertaste will be reduced or eliminated.

Stevia

Look for pure liquid stevia, pure powdered stevia, or powdered stevia with inulin; avoid stevia with maltodextrin, which is often used to bulk up stevia so that it matches the volume of sugar, cup for cup.

Erythritol

Erythritol is one of the sweeteners in Truvía (with rebiana, an isolate of stevia) and Swerve (with inulin). Avoid Pure Via, as it contains glucose and/or maltodextrin.

Xylitol

Xylitol is the most sugarlike of the chosen sweeteners: Unlike the others, it yields good glazing and streusel effects. Use it only in limited quantities, however, because it has a modest capacity to raise blood sugar. And dog owners should know that xylitol can be toxic to dogs.

Luo Han Guo/Monk Fruit

Monk fruit, a natural sweetener, is rapidly becoming a favorite because it lacks the bitter aftertaste that some people experience with stevia. Like stevia, it does not raise blood sugar or cause tooth decay, lacking the adverse health effects of conventional sweeteners. It's tough to find but becoming easier as demand increases. Avoid both Monk Fruit in the Raw and Nectresse because these products contain glucose and/or maltodextrin. Be sure to read packages and look for new products coming to supermarkets that contain just monk fruit or monk fruit and erythritol.

Sucralose

There is some uncertainty about the health implications of sucralose (a potential for allergy and idiosyncratic reactions; detrimental effects on bowel flora, at least in animal studies). It is also tough to obtain as pure sucralose without maltodextrin. (Splenda is sucralose with maltodextrin.) So this is the last choice among the sweeteners.

Your Shopping List

In addition to the real, single-ingredient foods that will become the focus of your diet, such as green peppers, onions, and other vegetables, as well as beef, pork, lamb, fish, chicken, and other meats, the following are common ingredients needed to follow the wheat-free lifestyle. This list includes just about everything you will need to make the meals in this cookbook.

Almond meal/flour

Almond milk, unsweetened

Baking powder (aluminum-free)

Cauliflower

Cheeses

Chia seeds, ground or whole

Chocolate—100% chocolate, 85% cocoa or greater

Chocolate chips, dark

Cocoa powder, unsweetened

Coconut, shredded and unsweetened; coconut flakes

Coconut flour

Coconut milk—canned for thickening recipes; carton for drinking

Cream of tartar

Dried fruit, unsweetened

Eggs

Extracts—natural almond, coconut, peppermint, and vanilla

Flaxseeds, preferably ground golden

Ground nut meals—ground almonds, hazelnuts, pecans, walnuts

Nut and seed butters—almond butter, peanut butter, sunflower seed butter

Nuts—raw almonds, Brazil nuts, hazelnuts, pecans, pistachios, walnuts; chopped pecans or walnuts for baking

Oils—avocado, coconut, extra-light olive, extra-virgin olive, flaxseed, walnut

Seeds—chia, raw pumpkin, raw sunflower, and sesame

Shirataki noodles (in the refrigerated section)

Spaghetti squash

Sweeteners—liquid stevia, powdered stevia (pure or with inulin, not maltodextrin), powdered erythritol, Truvía, xylitol, luo han guo/monk fruit

Zucchini

Replacement Ingredients for Other Food Sensitivities

A growing number of people have food sensitivities, allergic and otherwise, that make food choices tricky. While some, if not most, food sensitivities improve or disappear when wheat is removed from the diet (likely due to loss of the gliadin small bowel permeability effect), some people do indeed need to continue to avoid the source of their sensitivities.

Here is a starting list to identify potential replacement ingredients.

Replacement Ingredients for Other Food Sensitivities

If you are sensitive to:	Consider replacing with:
Almonds	Chia seed meal, garbanzo bean (chickpea) flour, pecan meal, pumpkin seed meal, sesame seed meal, sunflower seed meal, walnut meal
Butter	Avocado oil, coconut oil, extra-light olive oil, ghee (unless extremely dairy-sensitive), walnut oil
Eggs	Applesauce, chia seeds, coconut milk (canned variety), Greek yogurt (unsweetened), ground golden flaxseeds, pumpkin puree, tofu (from non-GMO soy)
Milk	Almond milk, coconut milk (carton variety), goat milk, hemp milk, soy milk (from non-GMO soy)
Nuts	Chia seeds, pumpkin seeds, sesame seeds, sunflower seeds
Peanut butter	Almond butter, hazelnut butter, sunflower seed butter
Sour cream	Coconut milk (canned variety)

Wheat . . . by Any Other Name!

Wheat is included in an astounding number of processed foods—because it stimulates appetite! Yes, those nice processed food manufacturers have had your number for many years. So recognizing the many varied names used for wheat products in food is essential to avoid inadvertent exposures.

It may be listed by obvious wheat labels, such as "wheat flour," "refined white flour," or "vital wheat gluten." Those are easy to spot. Consult this list for the not-so-obvious hidden sources that need to be watched out for too. They include:

Baguette

Barley

Beignet

Bran

Brioche

Bulgur

Burrito

Caramel coloring

Couscous

Crepe

Croutons

Durum

Einkorn

Emmer

Farina

Farro

Focaccia

Fu (gluten in Asian foods)

Gluten

Gnocchi

Graham flour

Gravy

Hydrolyzed vegetable protein

Hydrolyzed wheat starch

Kamut

Matzo

Modified food starch

Orzo

Panko (a bread crumb mixture used in Japanese cooking)

Ramen

Roux (wheat-based sauce or thickener)

Rusk

Rye

Seitan (nearly pure gluten used in place of meat)

Semolina

Soba (mostly buckwheat but usually also includes wheat)

Spelt

Strudel

Tabbouleh

Tart

Textured vegetable protein

Triticale

Triticum

Udon

Wheat bran

Wheat germ

Wraps

Don't commit this list to memory; simply reading through it will help you to recognize the varied ways wheat can infiltrate your food. Consult this list whenever uncertainty arises.

Kitchen Tools

None of the kitchen tools listed below are absolutely essential to get started on your wheat-free lifestyle—but they sure can simplify the process and save you a lot of time! I advise just getting started with your recipes, then add gadgets as the need arises.

For instance, spiral slicers make exquisite noodle replacements out of zucchini more consistently and more quickly than doing it with a knife. If you find you or your family really likes zucchini noodles, then it would be wise to invest in a Spiralizer or Spirelli device. Likewise, because I have yet to see a truly healthy ice cream in supermarket refrigerators, I offer a homemade version (page 222); a modern electric ice cream maker is therefore a huge time- and effort-saver.

Among the most useful devices:

Electric hand mixer

Food chopper/food processor—If you're in the market for one that is inexpensive and easy to use and clean up, the KitchenAid food chopper is my favorite for around $35.

Ice cream maker

Muffin cup liners (paper or silicone)

Muffin pan

Spiral slicer (Spiralizer or Spirelli)

Wooden picks

Tortilla press—Making a batch of tortillas to store for later use is much easier with this pressing device.

Waffle maker

Whoopie pan—Making perfect saucer-shaped whoopies or buns is much easier with these pans.

Ready, Set, Go!

If you've gotten this far, then you are well equipped to get started on your 30-minute wheat-free cooking adventure!

Note that, in addition to the single-dish recipes in the next several chapters, you will find an assortment of themed menus in the back of this book. I predict that you will discover just how rich, delicious, satisfying, and healthy this new wheat-free lifestyle can be!

MAKING THE WHEAT-FREE LIFESTYLE AS EASY AS 1, 2, 3!

FROM THE PERSPECTIVE of health and the way you feel, the wheat-free lifestyle blows away everything I have ever seen in my lifetime. Remove a dietary poison and appetite, health, and weight are transformed. The list of advantages gained by this wheat-free lifestyle ranges from head to toe, brain to bowels, appetite to sexual drive.

But there is one *disadvantage:* Because we have chosen to reject this common foodstuff, this creation of genetic manipulations, an ingredient in virtually all processed foods on supermarket shelves, we lose the *convenience* of prepared foods. We can no longer buy loaves of bread, bagels by the dozen, premade piecrusts, just-add-milk pancake mixes, or microwave-for-3-minute frozen dinners. For many people, those conveniences are a *big* part of their former diets.

Losing the convenience of processed foods means that we have to spend more time and effort creating basic foods, such as breads and salad dressings, from scratch. To economize on time and effort, however, I've created a number of mixes for baked goods, seasonings, and sauces and dressings. Once you've stocked up on these basic requirements, putting together quick meals becomes a snap.

Baking Mixes

Here are the basic recipes for mixes to make baked goods that are best prepared beforehand, then stored in the refrigerator for later use. For example, make up a batch of focaccia flatbread on the weekend, and then store it in the refrigerator to use for sandwiches over the course of the week.

Carb Watchers

All recipes in this cookbook were developed to be quick as well as to be strictly wheat-free. They were also designed to be healthy and to keep carbohydrate exposure low. Most of the recipes therefore provide a "net" carbohydrate content of no more than 15 grams per serving. Net carbohydrates are a very helpful idea conceived by the late low-carb guru, Dr. Robert Atkins, and are calculated by subtracting fiber from total carbohydrates, since fiber has virtually no glycemic potential:

Net carbohydrates = Total carbohydrates – Fiber

(There are some exceptions in the recipes that go just a bit higher in net carbohydrate exposure, especially some of the kid-friendly choices, since children are less susceptible to carbohydrate excesses than are adults. But *none* go substantially higher.)

All recipes, in addition to being wheat-free, are also free of other grains, contain little to no added sugars, use sugar and carbohydrate sources such as fruit sparingly, and likewise use starchy legumes as sparingly as possible.

ALL-PURPOSE BAKING MIX

PREP TIME: 5 MINUTES | **TOTAL TIME:** 5 MINUTES

Makes 5 cups

This mix is meant to be useful for creating a variety of different bread and baked goods recipes: loaf breads, flatbreads, rolls, scones, muffins, and cookies. Keeping a supply of this mix on hand will help save time in creating many of the 30-minute (or less!) meals.

4 cups almond meal/flour

1 cup ground golden flaxseeds

¼ cup coconut flour

2 teaspoons baking soda

1 teaspoon ground psyllium seed (optional)

In a large bowl, whisk together the almond meal/flour, flaxseeds, coconut flour, baking soda, and psyllium seed (if desired). Store in an airtight container, preferably in the refrigerator.

PER 1 TABLESPOON: 40 calories, 2 g protein, 2 g carbohydrates, 3 g total fat, 0 g saturated fat, 1 g fiber, 33 mg sodium

These restrictions are more important for adults (as opposed to growing children) who are trying to facilitate weight loss, trying to correct abnormal metabolic patterns such as high blood sugar or high triglycerides, or are just interested in maximizing the likelihood of ideal health.

In this cookbook, we also make use of the most benign sweeteners: stevia, monk fruit (luo han guo), erythritol, and xylitol. None have implications for tooth decay; none raise blood sugar when consumed in the modest quantities used in these recipes. Because there are substantial differences among these sweeteners (especially stevia preparations) from brand to brand, we did not specify any sweetener beyond saying, for instance, "sweetener equivalent to ½ cup sugar." This allows you to choose your favorite sweetener. It also means that the nutritional information for the carbohydrates contained in erythritol and xylitol are not listed in the nutritional information for each recipe, though, because of the minimal to no glycemic potential of these specific sugar alcohols, they act more like zero glycemic index sweeteners.

SANDWICH BREAD

PREP TIME: 5 MINUTES | **TOTAL TIME:** 45 MINUTES

Makes 1 loaf (16 slices)

This sandwich bread is one of the few recipes that fall outside of our 30-minute timeline, but if made ahead of time, it will allow you to create sandwiches and other dishes within that time limit.

3 cups All-Purpose Baking Mix (page 19)

1 teaspoon aluminum-free baking powder

½ teaspoon sea salt

5 eggs, separated

¼ cup butter or coconut oil, melted

1 tablespoon buttermilk or coconut milk (canned or carton variety)

Preheat the oven to 350°F. Grease an 8½" x 4½" loaf pan.

In a food processor, combine the baking mix, baking powder, and salt. Pulse until well blended. Add the egg yolks, butter or coconut oil, and buttermilk or coconut milk. Pulse until blended.

In a large bowl, with an electric mixer on high speed, beat the egg whites until soft peaks form. Pour into the flour mixture and pulse until the egg whites are evenly distributed, but do not run the machine at a constant speed. Spread into the pan and bake for 40 minutes, or until a wooden pick comes out clean.

PER SLICE: 174 calories, 7 g protein, 6 g carbohydrates, 15 g total fat, 4 g saturated fat, 3 g fiber, 234 mg sodium

BASIC FOCACCIA FLATBREAD

PREP TIME: 5 MINUTES | **TOTAL TIME:** 25 MINUTES

Makes 6 servings

One of the challenges of wheat-free baking with healthy substitute flours is generating vigorous "rise" in loaf-style breads, given the lack of yeast. In our Basic Focaccia Flatbread, we work around this limitation by making a flatbread—about as foolproof as a wheat-free bread gets.

This basic recipe is easily modified to create numerous variations. For example, add 2 teaspoons ground or crushed rosemary, 1 teaspoon dried oregano, and 1 teaspoon dried garlic for Italian-style flatbread. Or, after baking, brush the top with extra-virgin olive oil and sprinkle with grated Parmesan cheese. For bread that goes perfectly with cream cheese, add 1 teaspoon cinnamon and ½ teaspoon nutmeg and your choice of sweetener equivalent to 1 teaspoon sugar.

Note that the sequence of adding the ingredients specified below must be followed as written to avoid the common "baker's ammonia" effect, the result of the baking soda in the baking mix reacting with the proteins in the eggs, generating an ammonia smell, which is unpleasant. When you add the vinegar first, the acetic acid in the vinegar will react with the baking soda, preventing the reaction with the egg.

2 **cups All-Purpose Baking Mix (page 19)**

2 **tablespoons extra-virgin olive oil**

2 **tablespoons vinegar**

¼ **cup water**

1 **teaspoon xanthan gum (optional)**

½ **teaspoon sea salt**

3 **eggs, whisked**

Preheat the oven to 375°F. Grease a large rimmed baking sheet.

In a large bowl, place the baking mix. In a small bowl or cup, combine the oil, vinegar, water, xanthan gum (if desired), and salt. Add to the baking mix and quickly mix together. Let sit for 1 minute, then add the whisked eggs and mix together thoroughly.

With moistened hands, place the dough on the baking sheet and shape into an 8" × 12" rectangle.

Bake for 15 minutes, or until lightly browned. With a pizza cutter or knife, cut into six 3" × 4" pieces. Store in the refrigerator.

PER SERVING: 289 calories, 11 g protein, 10 g carbohydrates, 25 g total fat, 3 g saturated fat, 6 g fiber, 415 mg sodium

HERBED FOCACCIA FLATBREAD

PREP TIME: 15 MINUTES | **TOTAL TIME:** 35 MINUTES

Makes 6 servings

This flatbread proved a favorite among readers of my previous cookbook, providing a delicious way to enjoy Reuben sandwiches, ham and cheese sandwiches, smoked turkey sandwiches, or a wonderful bread to dip into extra-virgin olive oil. So I brought it back with some minor changes for the 30-minute experience.

Note that the sequence of adding the ingredients specified below must be followed as written to avoid the occasional "baker's ammonia" effect, the result of the baking soda in the baking mix reacting with the proteins in the eggs, generating an ammonia smell, which is unpleasant. When you add the vinegar first, the acetic acid in the vinegar will react with the baking soda, preventing the reaction with the egg.

1 cup shredded mozzarella or other cheese

3 cups All-Purpose Baking Mix (page 19)

1 teaspoon xanthan gum

1 teaspoon aluminum-free baking powder

1¼ teaspoons sea salt, divided

1 teaspoon onion powder

½ teaspoon garlic powder

1½ teaspoons dried rosemary, crushed

1½ teaspoons dried oregano

½ cup pitted black olives or kalamata olives, chopped or finely sliced

¼ cup sun-dried tomatoes, finely sliced

6 tablespoons extra-virgin olive oil, divided

2 tablespoons white vinegar or apple cider vinegar

2 eggs, separated

Preheat the oven to 375°F. Grease a baking sheet.

In a food chopper or food processor, pulse the cheese until reduced to small granules, about the size of couscous.

In a medium bowl, combine the processed cheese, baking mix, xanthan gum, baking powder, 1 teaspoon of the salt, the onion powder, garlic powder, rosemary, oregano, olives, and tomatoes. Mix well. Add 2 tablespoons of the oil and the vinegar and mix quickly. Set aside.

In a large bowl, with an electric mixer on high speed, beat the egg whites until stiff. Blend in the egg yolks and 2 tablespoons of the remaining oil at low speed. Pour into the reserved dough mixture and mix together with a spoon.

Place the dough onto the baking sheet and, using your hands, shape into an 11" × 12" rectangle. Alternately, cover the dough with parchment paper and use a rolling pin to roll the dough ½" thick.

Bake for 10 minutes. Remove from the oven and, using the blunt handle of a wooden spoon or other small rounded instrument, make small depressions in the surface every inch or so. Brush the surface with the remaining 2 tablespoons oil and sprinkle with the remaining ¼ teaspoon salt. Bake for 8 minutes, or until lightly browned.

Use a pizza cutter or knife to cut the flatbread into six 4" × 6" slices.

PER SERVING: 545 calories, 19 g protein, 19 g carbohydrates, 47 g total fat, 7 g saturated fat, 11 g fiber, 905 mg sodium

BASIC SANDWICH MUFFINS

PREP TIME: 5 MINUTES | TOTAL TIME: 20 MINUTES

Makes 4 halves or 2 complete

Put egg and sausage between 2 of these sandwich muffin halves and you have a breakfast muffin. Or use them for a mini hamburger.

To save time on busy days, make the muffins ahead of time. The recipe can, of course, be doubled or tripled to make larger batches. For delicious flavored muffins, add ¼ teaspoon each dried rosemary and dried oregano.

1 cup All-Purpose Baking Mix (page 19)

½ teaspoon aluminum-free baking powder

½ teaspoon sea salt

2 tablespoons extra-virgin olive oil

1 egg

1 tablespoon water + additional water if needed

Preheat the oven to 350° F. Grease 4 cups of a whoopie baking pan.

In a bowl, combine the baking mix, baking powder, and salt. Stir in the oil thoroughly. Add the egg and stir until mixed. If the dough is too stiff, add water 1 tablespoon at a time.

Divide the dough among the 4 whoopie cups. Using a spoon, flatten the mounds until approximately ½" thick, leaving a shallow well in the center. Bake for 12 minutes, or until the edges begin to brown. Allow to cool for 3 minutes before carefully removing from the pan.

PER SERVING (½ MUFFIN): 240 calories, 8 g protein, 8 g carbohydrates, 21 g total fat, 2 g saturated fat, 5 g fiber, 417 mg sodium

FLAXSEED WRAP BAKING MIX

PREP TIME: 5 MINUTES | **TOTAL TIME:** 5 MINUTES

Makes 2 cups

Ground golden flaxseeds make a wonderful wrap that can replace its wheat- or cornmeal-equivalent in any recipe.

2 cups ground golden flaxseeds

1 teaspoon aluminum-free
   baking powder

1½ teaspoons onion powder

1 teaspoon garlic powder

½ teaspoon sea salt

In a medium bowl, whisk together the flaxseeds, baking powder, onion powder, garlic powder, and salt. Store in an airtight container, preferably in the refrigerator.

PER ¼ CUP: 123 calories, 6 g protein, 9 g carbohydrates, 9 g total fat, 0 g saturated fat, 8 g fiber, 149 mg sodium

FLAXSEED WRAP

PREP TIME: 5 MINUTES | **TOTAL TIME:** 15 MINUTES

Makes 1

Here's one more workhorse recipe I've brought back from the original book. It has proven to be a perennial favorite, though this time made from our Flaxseed Wrap Baking Mix (page 25).

¼ cup Flaxseed Wrap Baking Mix (page 25)

1 teaspoon coconut oil, melted, or olive oil

1 egg

1 tablespoon water

In a medium bowl, combine the baking mix, oil, egg, and water until a thin, pourable dough forms.

Grease a microwaveable 9" glass or plastic pie plate. Pour the dough into the plate, using a spatula to empty the bowl. Tilt the plate to coat the bottom uniformly. Microwave on high power for 2 to 3 minutes, or until cooked. Let cool for 5 minutes. (Alternatively, bake in a greased ovenproof pie plate at 375°F for 10 minutes, or until the center is cooked.)

To remove the tortilla, lift up an edge with a spatula. If it sticks, use a pancake turner to gently loosen from the plate. Turn the wrap over and top with desired ingredients or store in the refrigerator for later use.

PER SERVING (1 WRAP): 234 calories, 12 g protein, 9 g carbohydrates, 18 g total fat, 6 g saturated fat, 8 g fiber, 220 mg sodium

PITA CHIPS

PREP TIME: 5 MINUTES | **TOTAL TIME:** 5 MINUTES

Makes 1 serving

By simply microwaving the ingredients for the Flaxseed Wrap a bit longer, you can easily create a bowl of crispy pita-like chips that can be dipped into fresh Guacamole (page 32) or Spicy Hummus (page 33). If you want more chips, work with 2 pie plates. That way, you can mix up a batch of batter while another batch cooks in the microwave.

¼ cup Flaxseed Wrap Baking Mix (page 25)

1 teaspoon coconut oil, melted, or olive oil

1 egg

1 tablespoon water

In a medium bowl, combine the baking mix, oil, egg, and water until a thin, pourable dough forms.

Grease a microwaveable 9" glass or plastic pie plate. Pour the dough into the plate, using a spatula to empty the bowl. Tilt the plate to coat the bottom uniformly. Microwave on high power for 3½ to 5 minutes, or until crispy. Break apart by hand into desired shape and size.

PER SERVING: 234 calories, 12 g protein, 9 g carbohydrates, 18 g total fat, 6 g saturated fat, 8 g fiber, 220 mg sodium

TORTILLA BAKING MIX

PREP TIME: 5 MINUTES | **TOTAL TIME:** 5 MINUTES

Makes 4¼ cups

This basic mix is suited to making up a batch of tortillas. Whip up, for example, 4 tortillas, and you will have enough to last almost a week in the refrigerator. You can quickly slap together a quesadilla or mini-pizza in a few minutes just by keeping some of these around and piling on a few ingredients.

3 cups ground golden flaxseeds

1 cup almond meal/flour

2 tablespoons onion powder

2 teaspoons garlic powder

1½ teaspoons sea salt

In a large bowl, whisk together the flaxseeds, almond meal/flour, onion powder, garlic powder, and salt. Store in an airtight container, preferably in the refrigerator.

PER ¼ CUP: 126 calories, 6 g protein, 8 g carbohydrates, 10 g total fat, 0 g saturated fat, 7 g fiber, 142 mg sodium

TORTILLAS

PREP TIME: 5 MINUTES | **TOTAL TIME:** 10 MINUTES

Makes 4

Here's how we put the Tortilla Baking Mix to work to yield 4 tortillas per batch.

1 cup Tortilla Baking Mix	**2 eggs**

Preheat the oven to 375°F. Line a large baking sheet with parchment paper.

Pour the baking mix into a large bowl. Whisk in the eggs until combined. Divide dough into 4 equal portions.

Roll each ball between 2 pieces of parchment paper until it is 6" in diameter. Alternatively (and much easier!), use a tortilla press lined with parchment paper.

Place on the baking sheet, with both pieces of parchment, and bake for 5 minutes, or until golden.

Store in the refrigerator.

PER SERVING (1 TORTILLA): 162 calories, 9 g protein, 8 g carbohydrates, 12 g total fat, 1 g saturated fat, 7 g fiber, 177 mg sodium

Sauces and Dressings

It happens with seasoning mixes, and it happens all too often with store-bought sauces and dressings: hidden wheat or other unhealthy ingredients. One common ingredient, for instance, in many salad dressings, virtually all barbecue sauces, ketchup, and other condiments, is high-fructose corn syrup. In fact, a quick examination of the labels at your local supermarket will show that there are very rare examples of truly healthy sauces and dressings!

So here is a collection of healthy, wheat-free, junk ingredient–free sauces and dressings that can help make interesting and delicious 30-minute (or less!) dishes!

BASIL PESTO

PREP TIME: 5 MINUTES | **TOTAL TIME:** 5 MINUTES

Makes ⅔ cup

I love growing my own basil plants and then picking the lushest leaves and grinding them into this fresh pesto, which bursts with the magical combination of olive oil, Parmesan cheese, and the basil. For especially delightful but simply elegant dishes, pour this on top of some shirataki noodles with an extra dash of sea salt and pepper, or add a couple of tablespoons to scrambled eggs (yes, the color is wacky, but it's delicious!).

1 cup packed fresh basil

2 tablespoons pine nuts

2 cloves garlic, chopped

⅓ cup extra-virgin olive oil

¼ cup grated Parmesan cheese

¼ teaspoon sea salt

1½ teaspoons white balsamic vinegar

In a food chopper or food processor, combine the basil, pine nuts, and garlic. Chop or process into a paste. Add the oil, cheese, salt, and vinegar and chop or process until the ingredients are blended and the pesto is bright green.

PER 1 TABLESPOON: 86 calories, 1 g protein, 1 g carbohydrates, 9 g total fat, 1.5 g saturated fat, 0 g fiber, 70 mg sodium

GUACAMOLE

PREP TIME: 10 MINUTES | TOTAL TIME: 10 MINUTES

Makes 6 servings

Here's something to dip your Pita Chips (page 27) into, or to spread on a wrap, tortilla, or sandwich. Guacamole is a satisfying and delicious dip for raw veggies, too.

3 ripe avocados, halved, pitted, and peeled

1 onion, coarsely chopped

1 serrano chile pepper, coarsely chopped (wear plastic gloves when handling)

2 cloves garlic, coarsely chopped

⅓ cup fresh cilantro, finely chopped

Juice of 1 lime

½ teaspoon sea salt

1 tomato, coarsely chopped

In a food chopper or food processor, combine the avocados, onion, pepper, garlic, cilantro, lime juice, and salt. Chop or pulse until slightly chunky and combined. Add the tomato and pulse until desired consistency.

PER SERVING: 129 calories, 2 g protein, 9 g carbohydrates, 11 g total fat, 1 g saturated fat, 5 g fiber, 140 mg sodium

SPICY HUMMUS

PREP TIME: 10 MINUTES | **TOTAL TIME:** 10 MINUTES

Makes 1¾ cups

Hummus is such a versatile dip and sandwich spread that I thought it would be best to provide a homemade, do-it-yourself version. It's also less costly making it yourself, rather than purchasing the deli version, which can get pretty pricey.

For a deeper, more mellow flavor, try roasting the garlic. Simply cut off and discard the top ½" of a whole garlic bulb, drizzle with ½ teaspoon olive oil, and wrap in foil. Bake in a 375°F oven for 40 to 45 minutes, or until the cloves are soft. Allow to cool for 20 minutes before squeezing the soft garlic cloves into the chickpea mixture.

If you don't like the taste of tahini, you can substitute toasted sesame oil or leave it out altogether.

¼ cup extra-virgin olive oil	½ teaspoon paprika
1 can (15.5 ounces) chickpeas, rinsed and drained	½ teaspoon sea salt
3–4 cloves garlic, minced	1 tablespoon grated Romano or Parmesan cheese (optional)
3 tablespoons lemon juice	1 tablespoon pine nuts (optional)
2 tablespoons tahini	1 tablespoon chopped chives (optional)
½ teaspoon ground red pepper (optional)	

In a food chopper or food processor, pulse the olive oil, chickpeas, and garlic. Add the lemon juice, tahini, red pepper (if desired), paprika, and salt and process until thoroughly mixed and smooth. Sprinkle with the cheese, pine nuts, or chives, if desired. Store in an airtight container in the refrigerator.

PER ¼ CUP: 118 calories, 3 g protein, 6 g carbohydrates, 10 g total fat, 1 g saturated fat, 1 g fiber, 179 mg sodium

MARINARA SAUCE

PREP TIME: 10 MINUTES | **TOTAL TIME:** 30 MINUTES

Makes 7 cups

As with other sauces and dressings, many store-bought marinara sauces contain added sugar or high-fructose corn syrup. The challenge in making it ourselves is keeping the time required down to our 30-minute maximum. Adding red wine to the sauce takes off the residual bitterness that ordinarily requires 2 hours of simmering on the stove to reduce. I keep a bottle of French Côtes du Rhône or bungundy, or a bottle of American Cabernet Sauvignon that has been open a bit too long to be drinkable, in the refrigerator for uses such as this.

2 tablespoons extra-virgin olive oil

2 shallots or 1 medium onion, finely chopped

3 garlic cloves, minced

1 teaspoon red-pepper flakes

2 cans (28 ounces each) diced tomatoes

1 can (6 ounces) tomato paste

2 tablespoons Italian Seasoning Mix* (page 56)

Sweetener equivalent to 1 tablespoon sugar

Sea salt and pepper to taste

¼ cup red wine

In a large saucepan over medium heat, heat the olive oil until hot. Cook the shallots, garlic, and pepper flakes until the shallots are translucent.

Meanwhile, pour the tomatoes into a blender and blend until you reach the desired consistency (the briefer the blending, the chunkier the sauce). Transfer the tomatoes to the saucepan. Stir in the tomato paste, seasoning mix, sweetener, salt, and pepper. Bring to a simmer over medium heat. Reduce the heat to low and simmer, stirring occasionally, for 20 minutes. Stir in the red wine and remove from the heat.

*Or substitute 2 teaspoons dried basil, 2 teaspoons dried oregano, 2 teaspoons dried rosemary.

PER ½ CUP: 74 calories, 2 g protein, 11 g carbohydrates, 2 g total fat, 0 g saturated fat, 2 g fiber, 261 mg sodium

BARBECUE SAUCE

PREP TIME: 5 MINUTES | **TOTAL TIME:** 25 MINUTES

Makes 3 cups

This variation on the perennial sauce favorite for meat fits perfectly into the wheat-free lifestyle. Slather it on ribs, steaks, pork, or fish for added spice and pizzazz.

3 cloves garlic, minced

1 tablespoon chili powder

1 tablespoon olive oil

1 can (28 ounces) tomato puree

2 tablespoons molasses

1 tablespoon apple cider vinegar

2 tablespoons mustard

½ teaspoon ground red pepper

½ teaspoon sea salt

1 tablespoon onion powder

Sweetener equivalent to ¼ cup sugar

In a medium saucepan over medium heat, cook the garlic and chili powder in the oil for 3 minutes. Add the tomato puree, molasses, vinegar, mustard, red pepper, salt, onion powder, and sweetener. Bring to a boil, reduce the heat to low, cover, and simmer for 15 minutes, stirring occasionally. Remove from the heat and cool before storing in the refrigerator.

PER ¼ CUP: 47 calories, 1 g protein, 9 g carbohydrates, 1 g total fat, 0 g saturated fat, 1 g fiber, 316 mg sodium

THAI RED CURRY SAUCE

PREP TIME: 5 MINUTES | **TOTAL TIME:** 5 MINUTES

Makes ¾ cup

Convert just about any meat or vegetable into a spicy, flavorful dish just by adding this Thai Red Curry Sauce.

1 **can (13.5 ounces) coconut milk**	¾ **teaspoon rice vinegar**
2 **tablespoons red curry paste**	¾ **teaspoon tamari**

In a small bowl, combine the coconut milk, curry paste, vinegar, and tamari. Stir until well mixed. Store in an airtight container in the refrigerator.

PER ¼ CUP: 269 calories, 3 g protein, 6 g carbohydrates, 27 g total fat, 24 g saturated fat, 2 g fiber, 477 mg sodium

GINGER-MISO SAUCE

PREP TIME: 5 MINUTES | **TOTAL TIME:** 5 MINUTES

Makes ½ cup

Here's an Asian spin on a sauce that can be used as a marinade or sauce for chicken or fish, as a unique alternative for barbecued ribs, or just as a salad dressing. Find miso paste in natural health food stores or Asian food markets.

1½ tablespoons miso paste

2 tablespoons sesame oil

1 tablespoon rice vinegar

1 teaspoon wasabi powder (optional)

1 teaspoon minced fresh ginger

½ teaspoon minced garlic (1 small clove)

1 teaspoon onion powder

2 tablespoons sesame seeds

¼ cup water

In a small bowl, whisk together the miso, sesame oil, vinegar, wasabi (if desired), ginger, garlic, onion powder, sesame seeds, and water until the miso is dissolved. Store in an airtight container in the refrigerator.

PER 1 TABLESPOON: 50 calories, 1 g protein, 1 g carbohydrates, 5 g total fat, 0.5 g saturated fat, 0 g fiber, 144 mg sodium

DILLED CUCUMBER YOGURT SAUCE

PREP TIME: 10 MINUTES | **TOTAL TIME:** 10 MINUTES

Makes 1⅓ cups

This easy sauce makes a delicious accompaniment to Middle Eastern Lamb Burgers (page 146).

1 cup whole milk plain Greek yogurt

½ cup peeled, grated English cucumber

2 tablespoons extra-virgin olive oil

1 tablespoon finely chopped fresh dill

1 teaspoon finely chopped fresh mint

¼ teaspoon garlic powder

½ teaspoon kosher salt

⅛ teaspoon ground black pepper

In a small bowl, combine the yogurt, cucumber, oil, dill, mint, garlic powder, salt, and pepper. Stir well.

PER ⅓ CUP: 99 calories, 6 g protein, 3 g carbohydrates, 7 g total fat, 1 g saturated fat, 0 g fiber, 242 mg sodium

TARTAR SAUCE

PREP TIME: 5 MINUTES | **TOTAL TIME:** 5 MINUTES

Makes ¾ cup

Simple and traditional, this version of Tartar Sauce is truly healthy!

½ cup olive oil mayonnaise

⅓ cup finely diced dill pickle

1 teaspoon dried onion

2 teaspoons lemon juice

In a small bowl, stir together the mayonnaise, pickle, dried onion, and lemon juice. Serve with fish.

PER 2 TABLESPOONS: 69 calories, 0 g protein, 1 g carbohydrates, 7 g total fat, 1 g saturated fat, 0 g fiber, 230 mg sodium

MAYONNAISE

PREP TIME: 5 MINUTES | TOTAL TIME: 10 MINUTES

Makes about 1¼ cups

Yes: Mayonnaise.

More and more people have come to me saying, "I don't trust the store-bought mayonnaise and all its peculiar ingredients. How do I make my own with healthy ingredients?"

Well, here you go!

All ingredients should be at room temperature. If any ingredients are cool or refrigerated, soak them in hot water until they're at room temperature before proceeding with the recipe. You can also add flavorings, such as paprika or dill, to the finished mayo.

3 egg yolks

2 teaspoons Dijon mustard

¼ teaspoon sea salt

2 cups extra-light olive oil

¼ cup white wine vinegar

....

In a food processor or with an electric mixer, combine the yolks, mustard, and salt. Pulse or blend at high speed. Slowly pour in the oil over several minutes and process or blend until the mixture thickens. Add the vinegar and process until combined.

Store in an airtight container in the refrigerator for up to 1 week.

PER 1 TABLESPOON: 102 calories, 0 g protein, 0 g carbohydrates, 12 g total fat, 2 g saturated fat, 0 g fiber, 26 mg sodium

GARLICKY MAYO SPREAD

PREP TIME: 5 MINUTES | **TOTAL TIME:** 5 MINUTES

Makes about 1 cup

Use this zesty spread on wheat-free sandwiches or to top the Salmon Croquettes (page 173).

1 cup Mayonnaise
(page 40)

1 tablespoon lemon juice

1 clove garlic, minced

⅛ teaspoon sea salt

⅛ teaspoon ground black pepper

In a small bowl, combine the mayonnaise, lemon juice, garlic, salt, and pepper. Stir until well blended. Store in an airtight container in the refrigerator.

PER 1 TABLESPOON: 101 calories, 0 g protein, 0 g carbohydrates, 11 g total fat, 1.5 g saturated fat, 0 g fiber, 102 mg sodium

SPICY CAJUN MAYO

PREP TIME: 5 MINUTES | **TOTAL TIME:** 5 MINUTES

Makes ½ cup

This flavorful mayo can serve as a spicy topping for sandwiches or wraps or as a unique dip for veggies. You can also add it to egg yolks to make quick but unique deviled eggs.

½ cup Mayonnaise (page 40)

1 teaspoon tomato paste

1 teaspoon lemon juice

¾ teaspoon Cajun Seasoning Mix (page 58)

In a small bowl, combine the mayonnaise, lemon juice, tomato paste, and seasoning mix. Stir well.

PER 1 TABLESPOON: 103 calories, 0 g protein, 0 g carbohydrates, 12 g total fat, 2 g saturated fat, 0 g fiber, 36 mg sodium

JAPANESE CARROT-GINGER DRESSING

PREP TIME: 10 MINUTES | **TOTAL TIME:** 10 MINUTES

Makes about 2 cups

If you've ever had a green salad at a Japanese restaurant, the greens themselves are not generally too impressive . . . but that carrot-ginger dressing? Wow! Well, here it is, re-created for you to enjoy on your salads at home.

You can do better than the iceberg lettuce typically used in Japanese restaurants. Instead, pair this dressing with varieties such as Boston, mizuna, purslane, and romaine. Arugula is especially delicious with this dressing.

3 large carrots, sliced

2 tablespoons coarsely chopped fresh ginger

1 shallot, coarsely chopped

½ cup extra-light olive oil or coconut oil

1 tablespoon toasted sesame oil

¼ cup rice vinegar

2 tablespoons water

1 tablespoon gluten-free soy sauce or miso paste

In a food processor or blender, combine the carrots, ginger, shallot, olive oil or coconut oil, sesame oil, vinegar, water, and soy sauce or miso paste. Pulse until reduced to a thin paste. Store in an airtight container in the refrigerator.

PER 2 TABLESPOONS: 80 calories, 0 g protein, 3 g carbohydrates, 8 g total fat, 1 g saturated fat, 1 g fiber, 127 mg sodium

HERBED RANCH DRESSING

PREP TIME: 5 MINUTES | **TOTAL TIME:** 5 MINUTES

Makes 2 cups

Store-bought mayonnaise is used in this recipe to simplify preparation. However, the quality of this ranch dressing will depend on the quality of the mayonnaise you choose. So be sure to choose brands that have no unhealthy ingredients, such as hydrogenated oils, or make your own (page 40). Thankfully, most mayonnaises are a simple combination of oils, eggs, vinegar, and seasonings. The oil used is usually the omega-6-rich soybean oil, but if you shop around, you can find brands made with olive oil and coconut oil. Alternatively, use conventional mayonnaise but replace one-third with your choice of healthy oil.

1   cup mayonnaise

½   cup sour cream

½   cup buttermilk

2   tablespoons lemon juice

¼   cup parsley, chopped

2   tablespoons chopped chives

¼   teaspoon dried dillweed

In a medium bowl, combine the mayonnaise, sour cream, buttermilk, lemon juice, parsley, chives, and dillweed. Mix well. Pour into a bottle or jar and store in the refrigerator.

PER 2 TABLESPOONS: 117 calories, 1 g protein, 1 g carbohydrates, 12 g total fat, 2 g saturated fat, 0 g fiber, 103 mg sodium

RANCH DRESSING

PREP TIME: 5 MINUTES | **TOTAL TIME:** 5 MINUTES

Makes about 2 cups

Back by popular demand, this ranch dressing recipe was included in the first two books. It has proven such a hit that I include it here, too.

1 cup sour cream	1½ teaspoons onion powder
½ cup mayonnaise	1 tablespoon white vinegar
½ cup Parmesan cheese	Pinch of sea salt
1 teaspoon garlic powder	1–2 tablespoons water

In a medium bowl, whisk together the sour cream, mayonnaise, cheese, garlic powder, onion powder, vinegar, salt, and 1 tablespoon of the water. If you prefer a thinner consistency, add the additional 1 tablespoon water. Pour into a bottle or jar and store in the refrigerator.

PER 2 TABLESPOONS: 53 calories, 1 g protein, 2 g carbohydrates, 5 g total fat, 2 g saturated fat, 0 g fiber, 104 mg sodium

CREAMY PESTO DRESSING

PREP TIME: 5 MINUTES | **TOTAL TIME:** 5 MINUTES

Makes ⅔ cup

This makes a great spread for sandwiches, as well as a dressing for green salads.

¼ cup sour cream

¼ cup buttermilk

3 tablespoons prepared basil pesto

1 tablespoon grated Romano cheese

In a small bowl, combine the sour cream, buttermilk, pesto, and cheese. Mix well. Pour into a bottle or jar and store in the refrigerator.

PER 2 TEASPOONS: 25 calories, 1 g protein, 1 g carbohydrates, 2 g total fat, 1 g saturated fat, 0 g fiber, 27 mg sodium

CREAMY TOMATO-CILANTRO DRESSING

PREP TIME: 5 MINUTES | **TOTAL TIME:** 5 MINUTES

Makes 1½ cups

This is a slightly different variation of traditional Thousand Island dressing. Like Thousand Island, it is also useful on sandwiches.

1 cup mayonnaise

½ cup tomato sauce

2 tablespoons chopped sun-dried tomatoes

1 tablespoon apple cider vinegar

⅓ cup chopped cilantro

¼ teaspoon ground black pepper

¼ teaspoon sea salt

In a small bowl, combine the mayonnaise, tomato sauce, sun-dried tomatoes, vinegar, cilantro, pepper, and salt. Stir until thoroughly mixed. Pour into a bottle or jar and store in the refrigerator.

PER 2 TABLESPOONS: 141 calories, 1 g protein, 2 g carbohydrates, 15 g total fat, 2 g saturated fat, 1 g fiber, 244 mg sodium

MOROCCAN DRESSING

PREP TIME: 5 MINUTES | **TOTAL TIME:** 5 MINUTES

Makes 1½ cups

The unique combination of spices in the Moroccan Seasoning Mix also makes a great salad dressing. Mediterranean salads with romaine lettuce, kalamata olives, and feta cheese go especially well with this dressing.

1 cup extra-virgin olive oil

½ cup vinegar (red wine, white wine, or apple cider)

4 teaspoons Moroccan Seasoning Mix (page 55)

Combine the oil, vinegar, and seasoning mix in a cruet or jar. Shake until mixed. Store in the refrigerator.

PER 1 TABLESPOON: 87 calories, 0 g protein, 0 g carbohydrates, 9 g total fat, 1.5 g saturated fat, 0 g fiber, 0 mg sodium

SPICY ITALIAN DRESSING

PREP TIME: 5 MINUTES | **TOTAL TIME:** 5 MINUTES

Makes 1½ cups

Once you make a batch of the Italian Seasoning Mix, there's no reason not to have a bottle of homemade Spicy Italian Dressing on hand, too!

1 cup extra-virgin olive oil

½ cup vinegar (red wine, white wine, balsamic, or white balsamic)

1 tablespoon Italian Seasoning Mix (page 56)

½ teaspoon sea salt

Combine the oil, vinegar, seasoning mix, and salt in a cruet or jar. Shake until mixed. Store in the refrigerator.

PER 1 TABLESPOON: 87 calories, 0 g protein, 0 g carbohydrates, 9 g total fat, 1 g saturated fat, 0 g fiber, 49 mg sodium

SUN-DRIED TOMATO ITALIAN DRESSING

PREP TIME: 5 MINUTES | **TOTAL TIME:** 5 MINUTES

Makes 1⅔ cups

This is a useful all-round, everyday salad dressing.

1 cup extra-virgin olive oil

¼ cup red wine vinegar

¼ cup water

¼ cup sun-dried tomatoes (oil-packed), chopped

2 teaspoons Italian Seasoning Mix (page 56)

2 tablespoons grated Romano cheese

In a blender, combine the oil, vinegar, water, tomatoes, seasoning mix, and cheese. Blend until thoroughly mixed. Pour into a bottle or jar and store in the refrigerator.

PER 2 TEASPOONS: 55 calories, 0 g protein, 0 g carbohydrates, 6 g total fat, 1 g saturated fat, 0 g fiber, 9 mg sodium

PLUM-CHIA JAM

PREP TIME: 5 MINUTES | **TOTAL TIME:** 15 MINUTES

Makes 2 cups

Choose the juiciest plums when they are ripe and slightly soft and they will yield a delicious jam when combined with the gel action of chia. Spread this treat on scones, a slice of Basic Focaccia Flatbread (page 21), or wheat-free pancakes.

4 plums	Sweetener equivalent to ¼ cup sugar
3 tablespoons ground chia seeds	1 tablespoon lemon juice

Pit the plums and coarsely chop. Place in a food chopper or food processor and pulse for 1 minute, or until reduced to a pulpy liquid.

In a medium bowl, combine the processed plums, chia seeds, sweetener, and lemon juice. Mix well. Set aside for 10 minutes. Store in an airtight container in the refrigerator. Stir prior to serving.

PER 2 TABLESPOONS: 26 calories, 1 g protein, 6 g carbohydrates, 1 g total fat, 0 g saturated fat, 1 g fiber, 0 mg sodium

STRAWBERRY BUTTER

PREP TIME: 5 MINUTES | **TOTAL TIME:** 10 MINUTES

Makes about 1 cup

This simple embellishment to butter yields a delightful spread for a slice of Sandwich Bread (page 20). It is easily modified by replacing the strawberries with other berries, such as cranberries (raw or cooked), fresh or dried apricots, or other fruit. Wrap a portion of the finished butter in plastic wrap, then foil, and it will keep in the freezer for 1 month.

½ cup fresh strawberries

½ cup butter, at room temperature

Sweetener equivalent to 2 tablespoons sugar

In a food chopper or food processor, pulse the strawberries briefly until they are finely chopped.

In a medium bowl, combine the strawberries, butter, and sweetener. Mix thoroughly. Alternatively, combine all of the ingredients in the bowl of a stand mixer and mix on low speed with the paddle attachment until thoroughly blended. Store in an airtight container in the refrigerator.

PER 1 TABLESPOON: 107 calories, 0 g protein, 2 g carbohydrates, 12 g total fat, 7 g saturated fat, 0 g fiber, 101 mg sodium

HERBED BUTTER

PREP TIME: 5 MINUTES | **TOTAL TIME:** 10 MINUTES

Makes 1 cup

Keeping a bit of this fragrant herbed butter on hand helps liven up vegetables, mashed cauliflower, chicken, beef, and fish with just a dollop. It can also be featured in a bowl at the table or formed (when semisolid) into any shape desired. I like keeping a variety of herbed and flavored butters stored in ramekins in the refrigerator. Change up the herbs, if desired; chives, sage, or thyme all work well. Wrap a portion of the finished butter in plastic wrap, then aluminum foil, and it will keep in the freezer for 1 month.

8 ounces butter, at room temperature

¼ cup chopped fresh basil, fresh rosemary, or fresh marjoram

½ teaspoon garlic powder or 1 teaspoon minced garlic

½ teaspoon sea salt

In a bowl, combine the butter, herb, garlic, and salt. Mix thoroughly. Alternatively, combine all the ingredients in the bowl of a stand mixer and mix on low speed with the paddle attachment until thoroughly blended. Store in an airtight container in the refrigerator.

PER 1 TABLESPOON: 102 calories, 0 g protein, 0 g carbohydrates, 12 g total fat, 7 g saturated fat, 0 g fiber, 150 mg sodium

Seasoning Mixes

Yes, even prepared seasoning mixes contain wheat—and maltodextrin and cornstarch and sugar and BHT (butylated hydroxytoluene) and other ingredients that add up to potential health issues . . . just from spices!

Single-ingredient herbs and spices, dried or fresh, are nearly always wheat-free and free of other undesirables. These recipes allow you to assemble your own healthy seasoning mixes that can be kept on hand to further trim time and effort off many recipes.

Many of the recipes in this book make use of these healthy seasoning mixes, untainted by unhealthy ingredients. Ideally, mix up a batch of each ahead of time to store on your shelves in an airtight container. Of course, if you find yourself going through your seasoning mixes quickly, double, triple, or otherwise multiply the ingredients to generate larger batches to store.

Since the calories and carbohydrates are negligible in these mixes, no nutritional information is included.

MOROCCAN SEASONING MIX

PREP TIME: 5 MINUTES | **TOTAL TIME:** 5 MINUTES

Makes ½ cup

2 tablespoons ground cumin

1 tablespoon ground coriander

2 teaspoons ground ginger

1½ teaspoons ground cinnamon

1 teaspoon ground red pepper

1 teaspoon ground cardamom

½ teaspoon ground cloves

1 teaspoon dried orange peel (optional)

In a small bowl, combine the cumin, coriander, ginger, cinnamon, red pepper, cardamom, cloves, and orange peel, if using. Store in an airtight container.

ITALIAN SEASONING MIX

PREP TIME: 5 MINUTES | **TOTAL TIME:** 5 MINUTES

Makes ⅓ cup

2 tablespoons dried basil

2 tablespoons dried oregano

2 tablespoons dried rosemary, crushed

1 tablespoon dried marjoram

1 tablespoon garlic powder

1 tablespoon onion powder

1 teaspoon ground black pepper

In a small bowl, combine the basil, oregano, rosemary, marjoram, garlic powder, onion powder, and pepper. Store in an airtight container.

TACO SEASONING MIX

PREP TIME: 5 MINUTES | **TOTAL TIME:** 5 MINUTES

Makes ⅓ cup

3 tablespoons chili powder

1½ tablespoons onion powder

2 teaspoons paprika

2 teaspoons garlic powder

1½ teaspoons ground red pepper

1½ teaspoons ground cumin

1 teaspoon dried oregano

In a small bowl, combine the chili powder, onion powder, paprika, garlic powder, red pepper, cumin, and oregano. Store in an airtight container.

CAJUN SEASONING MIX

PREP TIME: 5 MINUTES | **TOTAL TIME:** 5 MINUTES

Makes ⅓ cup

2 tablespoons paprika

1 tablespoon garlic powder

1 tablespoon onion powder

2 teaspoons ground black pepper

1½ teaspoons ground red pepper

1 teaspoon dried oregano

1 teaspoon dried thyme

½ teaspoon sea salt

In a small bowl, combine the paprika, garlic powder, onion powder, black pepper, red pepper, oregano, thyme, and sea salt. Store in an airtight container.

HERBES DE PROVENCE

PREP TIME: 5 MINUTES | **TOTAL TIME:** 5 MINUTES

Makes ⅓ cup

1 tablespoon dried savory

1 tablespoon dried rosemary, crushed

1 tablespoon dried thyme

1 tablespoon dried basil

1 tablespoon dried marjoram

1 tablespoon fennel seeds

1 teaspoon dried tarragon

In a small bowl, combine the savory, rosemary, thyme, basil, marjoram, fennel seeds, and tarragon. Store in an airtight container.

BREAKFASTS

POACHED EGGS OVER ROASTED ASPARAGUS

PREP TIME: 5 MINUTES | **TOTAL TIME:** 20 MINUTES

Makes 4 servings

In order to get plenty of green vegetables over the course of the day, it sure doesn't hurt to start with breakfast. Here is a poached egg dish served over asparagus and topped with an herbed butter. Chives were chosen, but parsley, rosemary, basil, and oregano—alone or in combination—also work well.

1 **bunch thin asparagus (1 pound), tough ends removed**

2 **tablespoons extra-virgin olive oil**

½ **teaspoon sea salt, divided**

6 **tablespoons butter**

2 **tablespoons finely chopped chives**

1 **tablespoon lemon juice**

2 **tablespoons white vinegar**

4 **eggs**

Ground black pepper

Preheat the oven to 400°F. On a large rimmed baking sheet, place the asparagus in a single layer. Drizzle with the oil and sprinkle with ¼ teaspoon of the salt. Roast for 13 minutes, or until lightly browned and tender.

Meanwhile, in a small saucepan over medium heat, melt the butter. Whisk in the chives, lemon juice, and the remaining ¼ teaspoon salt. Remove from the heat and set aside.

In a large skillet or saucepan over medium-high heat, heat 2" of water and the vinegar until simmering. Crack an egg into a small cup or bowl and gently slide out into the simmering water. Repeat with the remaining eggs. Simmer for 3 minutes, or until the whites are set and the yolks are slightly set but soft, or to desired doneness. An egg poacher can also be used.

Divide the asparagus evenly among 4 plates. Using a slotted spoon, carefully lift each egg out of the water, dabbing the bottom of the spoon on a paper towel to remove any excess water, and set on a plate on top of the asparagus. Drizzle with the reserved lemon-herb butter. Season with the pepper to taste.

PER SERVING: 311 calories, 9 g protein, 5 g carbohydrates, 29 g total fat, 14 g saturated fat, 2 g fiber, 422 mg sodium

BACON, EGG, AND TOMATO STACKS

PREP TIME: 5 MINUTES | **TOTAL TIME:** 15 MINUTES

Makes 4 servings

When you're in the mood for something a bit different from the usual scrambled or fried eggs, here is an easy 15-minute variation with tomato, Parmesan cheese, and bacon.

8 slices uncured bacon

1 large tomato, cut into four ½"-thick slices

1 tablespoon extra-virgin olive oil

¼ cup finely grated Parmesan cheese

4 eggs

3 tablespoons white vinegar

Sea salt

Ground black pepper

1 tablespoon snipped chives (optional)

Place the oven rack 6" from the heat source and preheat the broiler. Grease a baking sheet.

In a medium skillet over medium heat, cook the bacon for 5 minutes, or until desired level of doneness. Transfer to a plate lined with a paper towel.

Place the tomato slices in a single layer on the baking sheet. Drizzle with the oil and sprinkle each with 1 tablespoon of the cheese. Broil for 4 minutes, or until lightly browned. Set aside.

In a large skillet or saucepan over medium heat, heat 2" of water and the vinegar until simmering. Crack each egg into a separate small custard cup or bowl. Gently add each egg, one at a time, to the simmering water. Cook for 3 to 4 minutes for soft set, 5 minutes for medium set, or 7 minutes for hard set.

Place 2 slices of bacon crisscross on top of each broiled tomato. When the eggs are cooked, use a slotted spoon to carefully lift them out of the water, dabbing the bottom of the spoon on a paper towel to remove any excess water. Place on top of the tomato and bacon stacks. Season with the salt and pepper to taste. Top with chives, if desired.

PER SERVING: 253 calories, 23 g protein, 2 g carbohydrates, 20 g total fat, 8 g saturated fat, 1 g fiber, 950 mg sodium

HUEVOS RANCHEROS OVER
PAN-FRIED QUESO BLANCO

PREP TIME: 5 MINUTES | TOTAL TIME: 15 MINUTES

Makes 4 servings

Queso blanco is a firm, mild fresh cheese, similar in texture to farmer cheese, and sold in most supermarkets. Its unique quality is that it browns and softens without melting or losing shape. It should not be confused with queso fresco, which is more of a "crumbly" fresh cheese, much like feta.

8 ounces queso blanco cheese, cut into four ½"-thick slices

2 tablespoons butter

4 eggs

¼ teaspoon sea salt

½ cup salsa

1 large avocado, halved, pitted, peeled, and diced

Coat a medium skillet with olive oil cooking spray and heat over medium-high heat. Add the cheese slices and cook for 2 minutes, or until golden brown. Turn and cook for 1 minute to brown the other side. Transfer to a plate lined with a paper towel.

Reduce the heat to medium. Add the butter to the skillet. When the butter begins to sizzle, break the eggs into the skillet, and cook for 4 minutes, or until the whites are set and the yolks are the desired doneness. Season with the salt.

To assemble, place the fried eggs on top of the cheese slices. Top with the salsa and avocado.

PER SERVING: 356 calories, 19 g protein, 5 g carbohydrates, 30 g total fat, 14 g saturated fat, 2 g fiber, 682 mg sodium

MEDITERRANEAN SCRAMBLE

PREP TIME: 10 MINUTES | **TOTAL TIME:** 20 MINUTES

Makes 4 servings

To bring out the full, rich character of this healthy Mediterranean egg dish, use pasture-raised eggs whenever possible, the kind with orange-colored yolks that burst with flavor.

- 4 tablespoons extra-virgin olive oil, divided
- 8 ounces Italian sausage, thinly sliced
- 1 small onion, finely chopped
- 2 cloves garlic, minced
- 1 can (14 ounces) quartered artichoke hearts, drained and chopped
- ¼ cup sun-dried tomatoes, finely chopped
- ¼ cup pitted kalamata olives, sliced
- 8 eggs
- ½ cup crumbled feta cheese

In a large skillet over medium heat, heat 2 tablespoons of the oil. Cook the sausage for 3 minutes, or until starting to brown. Add the onion and garlic and cook, stirring occasionally, for 3 minutes, or until the onion is soft and the sausage is no longer pink.

Stir in the remaining 2 tablespoons oil, the artichokes, tomatoes, and olives. In a medium bowl, whisk the eggs and pour into the skillet. Cook for 4 minutes, stirring occasionally, or until the eggs are set. Remove from the heat and gently stir in the cheese.

PER SERVING: 621 calories, 27 g protein, 14 g carbohydrates, 51 g total fat, 15 g saturated fat, 2 g fiber, 1,467 mg sodium

MINI QUICHE LORRAINES

PREP TIME: 5 MINUTES | **TOTAL TIME:** 25 MINUTES

Makes 2 servings

This is a unique interpretation of a wheat-free "quiche," a variation of a traditional German-French dish that retains the essential flavor and feel of real cream. For a dairy-free version, you can replace the cream with coconut milk.

- 2 ounces pancetta, finely diced
- 2 tablespoons almond meal/flour
- ¼ teaspoon aluminum-free baking powder
- 2 eggs

- ⅓ cup cream or half-and-half
- 2 tablespoons finely minced chives or scallion tops
- ⅛ teaspoon ground black pepper

Preheat the oven to 350°F. Grease a 12-cup mini-muffin pan.

In a small skillet over medium heat, cook the pancetta for 5 minutes, or until lightly browned.

In a small bowl, whisk together the almond meal/flour and baking powder. In another small bowl, combine the eggs, cream or half-and-half, chives or scallion tops, and pepper and beat lightly. Stir the flour mixture into the egg mixture until combined. Divide the pancetta among the muffin cups. Divide the batter evenly among the muffin cups (cups will be almost full).

Bake for 12 minutes, or until puffed and light golden. Cool for 5 minutes on a rack. Remove from the pan.

PER 6 MINI QUICHES: 351 calories, 14 g protein, 3 g carbohydrates, 32 g total fat, 14 g saturated fat, 1 g fiber, 670 mg sodium

CHORIZO FRITTATA

PREP TIME: 10 MINUTES | **TOTAL TIME:** 30 MINUTES

Makes 8 servings

Using chorizo sausage in this frittata saves you the effort of adding spices and flavorings—because they're already in the sausage! Combine the spice of chorizo with the healthy green of kale and you have a perfect, healthy combination that is filling. Make the frittata ahead of time, refrigerate it, and eat it over the course of the week for an entire week's worth of healthy breakfasts.

2 tablespoons coconut oil

6 ounces chorizo sausage, chopped

1 yellow onion, chopped

2 cloves garlic, minced

8 ounces fresh or frozen, thawed kale, chopped

½ cup sun-dried tomatoes, coarsely chopped

½ cup sliced baby bella mushrooms

10 eggs

½ teaspoon sea salt

Preheat the oven to 375°F.

In a large ovenproof skillet over medium-high heat, heat the oil. Cook the sausage, onion, and garlic for 3 minutes, or until the sausage is barely pink and the onion begins to soften. Reduce the heat to medium. Stir in the kale, tomatoes, and mushrooms. Cover and cook, stirring frequently, for 4 minutes, or until the mushrooms are tender.

Meanwhile, in a medium bowl, whisk the eggs and salt. Add to the skillet and gently tilt to distribute the eggs. Cook for 2 minutes, or until the bottom and edges of the egg mixture become slightly firm. Transfer to the oven and bake for 10 minutes, or until the center is nearly set.

PER SERVING: 247 calories, 15 g protein, 7 g carbohydrates, 18 g total fat, 8 g saturated fat, 1 g fiber, 470 mg sodium

CRAB-ASPARAGUS FRITTATA

PREP TIME: 10 MINUTES | TOTAL TIME: 30 MINUTES

Makes 8 servings

Here's about as nutritionally complete a breakfast as you could find! No junk breakfast cereal ingredients here: no sugar, no cornstarch, no wheat—just satisfying, healthy foods that have no adverse health effects.

8 eggs

¾ cup cream or coconut milk (canned or carton)

10 stalks asparagus, sliced diagonally into ¾" segments

1 can (6 ounces) crabmeat, drained

4 tablespoons extra-virgin olive oil, divided

1 small yellow onion, finely chopped

2 cloves garlic, minced

½ teaspoon sea salt

Preheat the oven to 375°F.

In a large bowl, whisk the eggs. Add the cream or coconut milk, asparagus, crabmeat, and 2 tablespoons of the oil. Whisk to combine. Set aside.

In a large ovenproof skillet over medium heat, heat the remaining 2 tablespoons oil until hot. Cook the onion and garlic for 3 minutes, or until the onion is soft. Sprinkle with the salt. Pour the reserved egg mixture into the skillet and stir to combine. Cook for 3 minutes, or until the edges begin to firm. Transfer to the oven and bake for 10 minutes, or until a knife inserted in the center comes out clean.

PER SERVING: 234 calories, 10 g protein, 3 g carbohydrates, 20 g total fat, 8 g saturated fat, 1 g fiber, 290 mg sodium

MINI BAKED EGG CASSEROLES

PREP TIME: 5 MINUTES | **TOTAL TIME:** 25 MINUTES

Makes 4 servings

Canadian bacon, Cheddar cheese, and eggs are combined in this baked breakfast treat. If you've got some on hand, toast made with Sandwich Bread (page 20) and spread with some butter would be perfect!

8 slices Canadian bacon

½ cup shredded Cheddar cheese

8 eggs

2 tablespoons finely chopped chives or scallion tops (optional)

Preheat the oven to 350°F. Lightly coat 8 muffin cups with cooking spray or oil.

Line each muffin cup with 1 slice of the Canadian bacon. Place 1 tablespoon of the cheese in the bottom of each. Carefully break 1 egg into each muffin cup.

Bake for 15 minutes, or until just set and the whites are cooked but the yolks are still soft. Sprinkle with the chives or scallion tops, if desired. Let stand for 5 minutes before removing from the cups and serving.

PER SERVING: 247 calories, 22 g protein, 1 g carbohydrates, 16 g total fat, 7 g saturated fat, 0 g fiber, 499 mg sodium

BREAKFAST CRAB CAKES

PREP TIME: 5 MINUTES | **TOTAL TIME:** 15 MINUTES

Makes 4 servings

These simple crab cakes help jazz up fried eggs, while adding the healthy nutrition of seafood to breakfast.

In place of the Italian Seasoning Mix, you can substitute ½ teaspoon dried oregano and ½ teaspoon dried basil.

1 can (6 ounces) crabmeat, drained	2 teaspoons extra-virgin olive oil
¼ cup ground golden flaxseeds	½ teaspoon sea salt
1 teaspoon Italian Seasoning Mix (page 56)	2 tablespoons butter
5 eggs	

Preheat the oven to 375°F.

In a medium bowl, combine the crabmeat, flaxseeds, and seasoning mix. Whisk in 1 egg, oil, and salt.

Divide into four 3" patties and place in a shallow baking pan. Bake for 10 minutes, or until cooked through and slightly firm.

Meanwhile, in a large skillet over medium-high heat, melt the butter. Crack the remaining 4 eggs into the skillet and cook for 2 minutes, or until the whites begin to set. Turn over the eggs and cook for 2 minutes, or until the yolks are set.

Place each crab cake on a plate and top each with a fried egg.

PER SERVING: 228 calories, 17 g protein, 3 g carbohydrates, 17 g total fat, 6 g saturated fat, 2 g fiber, 504 mg sodium

PECAN-PUMPKIN HOTCAKES

PREP TIME: 5 MINUTES | **TOTAL TIME:** 20 MINUTES

Makes 8

Serve these fluffy, fragrant hotcakes with whipped cream, pumpkin butter, or a no-sugar-added berry jam. Alongside some bacon or sausage, you've got a perfect breakfast!

1 teaspoon ground cinnamon	1 cup almond butter, melted
½ teaspoon ground nutmeg	1 cup pumpkin puree
¼ cup finely chopped pecans	1 teaspoon vanilla extract
Sweetener equivalent to ¼ cup sugar	2 eggs
1 teaspoon baking soda	

Preheat the oven to 350°F. Line a shallow baking pan with parchment paper.

In a large bowl, combine the cinnamon, nutmeg, pecans, sweetener, and baking soda and mix well. Stir in the almond butter, pumpkin, and vanilla. In a small bowl, whisk the eggs and then stir into the mixture.

For each hotcake, scoop ⅓ cup of the batter onto the baking pan. Bake for 12 minutes, or until slightly firm to the touch and a wooden pick inserted in the center comes out clean.

PER 1 HOTCAKE: 246 calories, 9 g protein, 9 g carbohydrates, 21 g total fat, 3 g saturated fat, 5 g fiber, 248 mg sodium

GINGERBREAD BREAKFAST CAKES

PREP TIME: 5 MINUTES | **TOTAL TIME:** 25 MINUTES

Makes 6

These cakes taste like gingerbread cookies and will delight big and little kids: They'll feel like they're having dessert for breakfast! Minus wheat and sugar, these healthy cakes have no nutritional downside.

Spread cream cheese, butter, or Plum-Chia Jam (page 51) over the top.

2 **cups All-Purpose Baking Mix (page 19)**

1 **teaspoon aluminum-free baking powder**

1 **teaspoon ground ginger**

¾ **teaspoon ground cinnamon**

¼ **teaspoon ground nutmeg**

¼ **teaspoon ground cloves**

Sweetener equivalent to ½ cup sugar

1 **teaspoon lemon juice**

¼ **cup warm water**

1 **tablespoon molasses**

1 **egg, whisked**

Preheat the oven to 350°F. Line a baking sheet with parchment paper.

In a medium bowl, combine the baking mix, baking powder, ginger, cinnamon, nutmeg, cloves, and sweetener and mix thoroughly.

In a small bowl, combine the lemon juice and water. Pour into the dry mixture, add the molasses, and mix. Wait for 1 minute, and then stir in the egg.

Spoon out the dough in 6 mounds onto the baking sheet, pressing down to flatten to ¾" thickness. Bake for 15 minutes, or until a wooden pick inserted in the center comes out clean.

PER 1 CAKE: 236 calories, 9 g protein, 13 g carbohydrates, 18 g total fat, 2 g saturated fat, 6 g fiber, 270 mg sodium

SILVER DOLLAR PANCAKES

PREP TIME: 5 MINUTES | **TOTAL TIME:** 25 MINUTES

Makes 24

These pancakes are lightly sweetened and are delicious with or without syrup.

The more fragile structure yielded by the wheat-free almond meal/flour and coconut flour makes better small pancakes, thus the 3" diameter suggested here.

¼ cup almond meal/flour

¼ cup coconut flour

1 teaspoon baking soda

Sweetener equivalent to
1 tablespoon sugar

¼ cup finely chopped walnuts

½ teaspoon ground cinnamon

3 eggs

½ cup no-sugar-added applesauce

5 tablespoons water

2 tablespoons butter or coconut oil,
melted, or extra-light olive oil

In a medium bowl, whisk together the almond meal/flour, coconut flour, baking soda, sweetener, walnuts, and cinnamon.

In a large bowl, whisk together the eggs, applesauce, water, and butter or oil. Add to the flour mixture and whisk just until combined.

Lightly grease a large skillet or griddle and heat over medium-low heat until hot. For each 3" pancake, pour 1 tablespoon batter onto the skillet. Cook for 2 minutes, or until small bubbles form on top and the edges are cooked and lightly browned. Carefully turn and cook for 2 minutes, or until golden on the bottom. Repeat with the remaining batter.

PER 6 PANCAKES: 236 calories, 8 g protein, 10 g carbohydrates, 19 g total fat, 6.5 g saturated fat, 4 g fiber, 438 mg sodium

BREAKFAST CHEESECAKE

PREP TIME: 10 MINUTES | TOTAL TIME: 30 MINUTES + COOLING TIME

Makes 8 servings

Yes, cheesecake for breakfast! Made ahead of time, this simple and light cheesecake can be a special treat to start your morning. Because it is made with ricotta, rather than cream cheese, this Breakfast Cheesecake is lighter in texture than standard cheesecake. And it's not just for breakfast; this recipe can serve as a light dessert, too.

If desired, top with Strawberry Glaze (page 216) or Plum-Chia Jam (page 51).

1 cup ricotta cheese, at room temperature

½ cup coconut flour

Sweetener equivalent to ¾ cup sugar

4 teaspoons lemon juice

4 eggs, separated

1 teaspoon vanilla extract

Preheat the oven to 375°F. Grease a 9" x 9" baking pan.

In a medium bowl, place the cheese, flour, sweetener, lemon juice, egg yolks, and vanilla.

In another medium bowl, with an electric mixer on high speed, beat the egg whites until stiff peaks form. Using the same beaters, beat the cheese mixture until smooth. With a spoon, gently fold the egg whites into the cheese mixture until thoroughly combined.

Pour into the baking pan. Bake for 20 minutes, or until the edges begin to brown and a wooden pick inserted in the center comes out clean. Cool slightly before serving.

PER SERVING: 122 calories, 8 g protein, 5 g carbohydrates, 7 g total fat, 4.5 g saturated fat, 3 g fiber, 77 mg sodium

BREAKFAST COOKIES

PREP TIME: 10 MINUTES | **TOTAL TIME:** 25 MINUTES

Makes 12 cookies

"Breakfast" and "cookies" ordinarily don't belong together . . . unless we replace all of the unhealthy ingredients with healthy ingredients! Because these cookies are mostly made of nuts, coconut, egg, and apple, they are perfectly healthy and compatible with any breakfast.

I use dried apples for sweetness, which is a way to obtain just a bit of natural sweetness but with less sugar exposure than from other dried fruits, such as raisins or dates.

2 cups All-Purpose Baking Mix (page 19)

1 teaspoon ground cinnamon

¼ teaspoon sea salt

Sweetener equivalent to ½ cup sugar

½ cup unsweetened coconut flakes

½ cup chopped walnuts

½ cup chopped dried apples

½ cup whole milk plain Greek yogurt

2 tablespoons butter, melted

1 egg

1 teaspoon vanilla extract

Preheat the oven to 350°F. Line a baking sheet with parchment paper.

In a large bowl, combine the baking mix, cinnamon, salt, sweetener, coconut, walnuts, and dried apples.

In a small bowl, combine the yogurt and butter. Add the egg and vanilla and mix well. Pour into the flour mixture and stir until well combined. The dough will be thick. Use a cookie scoop or tablespoon to form balls consisting of 3 tablespoons each and place on the baking sheet. Lightly wet your hands and use your palms or a large spoon to flatten to ½" thickness.

Bake for 13 minutes, or until golden. The cookies will be soft. Let cool slightly before transferring to a rack to cool completely.

PER 1 COOKIE: 204 calories, 7 g protein, 10 g carbohydrates, 17 g total fat, 4.5 g saturated fat, 4 g fiber, 160 mg sodium

CINNAMON-PECAN SCONES

PREP TIME: 10 MINUTES | **TOTAL TIME:** 25 MINUTES + COOLING TIME

Makes 8 scones

Whip up a batch or two of these Cinnamon-Pecan Scones to eat over the course of the week for a quick, filling, and healthy breakfast. Optionally, top with Plum-Chia Jam (page 51).

2 cups All-Purpose Baking Mix (page 19)

3 tablespoons coconut flour

½ teaspoon sea salt

1½ teaspoons ground cinnamon

¼ cup coconut oil, cold

Sweetener equivalent to ¼ cup sugar

¼ cup chopped pecans

¼ cup buttermilk or canned coconut milk

1 egg

Preheat the oven to 350°F. Line a baking sheet with parchment paper.

In a large bowl, combine the baking mix, coconut flour, salt, and cinnamon. Using a pastry cutter, cut the oil into the flour mixture for 1 minute, or until incorporated and the mixture resembles damp sand. Stir in the sweetener, pecans, buttermilk or coconut milk, and egg, mixing just until blended. The dough will be thick and stiff.

Use a cookie scoop or tablespoon to scoop the dough and loosely shape it into 8 equal balls. Place 2" apart on the baking sheet. Use your hands or a large spoon to lightly flatten to ½" thickness. Bake for 13 minutes, or until lightly browned around the edges. Remove to a rack and cool for 5 minutes.

PER 1 SCONE: 265 calories, 8 g protein, 10 g carbohydrates, 24 g total fat, 8 g saturated fat, 6 g fiber, 258 mg sodium

PESTO BREAKFAST BISCUITS

PREP TIME: 5 MINUTES | **TOTAL TIME:** 20 MINUTES

Makes 4 biscuits

Alongside some scrambled or fried eggs, these savory pesto biscuits round out a healthy breakfast, complete with plenty of olive oil, nuts, and cheese. If you don't have time to make homemade pesto, you can substitute your favorite store-bought brand.

1 cup All-Purpose Baking Mix (page 19)

½ cup coconut flour

2 tablespoons ground golden flaxseeds

1 teaspoon aluminum-free baking powder

2 tablespoons grated Parmesan cheese

¼ cup water

1 tablespoon vinegar

1 egg

2–4 tablespoons Basil Pesto (page 31)

Preheat the oven to 375°F. Line a baking sheet with parchment paper.

In a medium bowl, combine the baking mix, coconut flour, flaxseeds, baking powder, and cheese. Stir in the water and vinegar, then allow to sit for 1 minute.

Mix in the egg and pesto, combining thoroughly. The mixture will be very stiff.

Spoon out the dough onto the baking sheet in four ¼"-thick mounds. Bake for 15 minutes, or until firm to the touch.

PER BISCUIT: 305 calories, 12 g protein, 17 g carbohydrates, 23 g total fat, 5 g saturated fat, 11 g fiber, 369 mg sodium

HERBED BISCUITS AND GRAVY

PREP TIME: 10 MINUTES | TOTAL TIME: 25 MINUTES

Makes 10 servings

Biscuits and gravy: the ultimate comfort food . . . one you thought you'd never have again!

The familiar dish of breakfast and holiday meals is re-created here with delicious gravy that you can pour over hot biscuits. Because it contains no wheat or other unhealthy thickeners, such as cornstarch, there should be no blood sugar or insulin issues with this dish, nor joint pain, edema, acid reflux, mind "fog," or dandruff. Life is good without wheat!

While the gravy is also dairy-free for those with dairy intolerances, the biscuits are not, as they contain both cheese and butter. For dairy-free biscuits, omit the cheese and replace the butter with oil, such as coconut, extra-light olive, or walnut.

BISCUITS

- 1 cup shredded Cheddar cheese
- 2 cups All-Purpose Baking Mix (page 19)
- 1 teaspoon dried basil
- 1 teaspoon dried rosemary, crushed
- ¾ teaspoon baking soda
- ½ teaspoon sea salt
- 2 eggs
- ½ cup butter or coconut oil, melted, or extra-virgin olive oil

GRAVY

- 2 tablespoons extra-virgin olive oil
- 1 pound ground loose sausage
- 1¾ cups beef broth
- ¼ cup coconut flour
- ¼ cup canned coconut milk
- ½ teaspoon onion powder
- ½ teaspoon garlic powder
- ½ teaspoon sea salt

Preheat the oven to 375°F. Line a baking sheet with parchment paper

To make the biscuits: In a food chopper or food processor, pulse the cheese to a fine, granular consistency. Transfer to a large bowl and add the baking mix, basil, rosemary, baking soda, and salt. Mix thoroughly. Add the eggs and butter or oil and mix thoroughly. The dough will be thick.

Spoon out the dough onto the baking sheet in ten 4" rounds. Bake for 10 minutes, or until lightly browned and a wooden pick inserted in the center of a biscuit comes out clean.

To make the gravy: While the biscuits are baking, in a large skillet over medium heat, heat the oil. Cook the sausage, breaking it up as it browns, for 8 minutes, or until no longer pink. Transfer to a plate and set aside.

Return the skillet to the heat and increase to medium-high. Heat the broth until nearly boiling. Reduce the heat to medium-low. Whisk in the flour a teaspoon at a time, over 5 minutes (stop adding when the gravy obtains the desired thickness). Pour in the coconut milk and stir well. Add the onion powder, garlic powder, and salt. Return the reserved sausage to the skillet and simmer over low heat for 5 minutes. Add additional salt to taste.

Ladle the gravy onto the biscuits just before serving.

PER SERVING: 457 calories, 17 g protein, 8 g carbohydrates, 41 g total fat, 15 g saturated fat, 5 g fiber, 976 mg sodium

STRAWBERRY-COCONUT BISCUITS

PREP TIME: 10 MINUTES | **TOTAL TIME:** 30 MINUTES

Makes 20 biscuits

All right, I may have pushed the 30-minute time envelope here just by a bit . . . but it is so worth it! These biscuits are exceptionally tasty and deliciously crumbly with a streusel-like surface. Your family will surely forgive you the extra 5 or so minutes!

¼ cup ground golden flaxseeds

¾ cup cold water

1 cup coconut flour

½ cup shredded unsweetened coconut

Sweetener equivalent to 2 tablespoons sugar

1 teaspoon baking soda

¼ teaspoon sea salt

¾ cup strawberries, finely chopped

½ cup coconut oil, melted

1 egg

Preheat the oven to 375°F. Line a baking sheet with parchment paper.

In a small mug or bowl, combine the flaxseeds and water and stir briefly. Place in the freezer for 5 minutes.

Meanwhile, in a large bowl, combine the flour, coconut, baking soda, salt, and strawberries. Mix well. Stir in the oil and combine thoroughly.

Remove the flaxseed mixture from the freezer and whisk in the egg. Stir into the flour mixture. The dough will be somewhat stiff. Use a cookie scoop or tablespoon to scoop the dough onto the baking sheet.

Bake for 17 minutes, or until a wooden pick inserted in the center of a biscuit comes out clean.

PER BISCUIT: 101 calories, 2 g protein, 5 g carbohydrates, 9 g total fat, 7 g saturated fat, 3 g fiber, 99 mg sodium

STRAWBERRY-PEANUT BUTTER PARFAITS

PREP TIME: 10 MINUTES | TOTAL TIME: 10 MINUTES

Makes 4 servings

The flavor of these parfaits is reminiscent of a peanut butter and strawberry jam sandwich. They can easily be made ahead of time in portable containers and eaten on the go or packed to take along with you.

2 cups whole milk plain Greek yogurt	1 teaspoon vanilla extract
¼ cup natural no-sugar-added peanut butter	2 tablespoons ground golden flaxseeds
¼ cup cream	1 cup sliced strawberries
Sweetener equivalent to ¼ cup sugar	¼ cup lightly salted roasted peanuts, chopped

In a medium bowl, combine the yogurt and peanut butter, mixing until blended. Stir in the cream, sweetener, vanilla, and flaxseeds and mix well. In 2 small bowls or parfait glasses, spoon one-quarter of the yogurt mixture and top with half of the strawberries. Divide the remaining yogurt mixture between the 2 bowls. Top with the remaining strawberries and the peanuts.

PER SERVING: 301 calories, 18 g protein, 15 g carbohydrates, 19 g total fat, 5 g saturated fat, 4 g fiber, 127 mg sodium

KEFIR SMOOTHIES

Each recipe yields approximately 1¼ cups. All recipes, of course, can be doubled or tripled to make a batch that will last several days in the refrigerator.

PREP TIME: 5 MINUTES | **TOTAL TIME:** 5 MINUTES

KID-FRIENDLY

PIÑA COLADA SMOOTHIE

Makes 1 serving

A healthy breakfast or snack, the tropical flavors of this piña colada smoothie will persuade any spouse or child that the wheat-free lifestyle is every bit as interesting as a wheat-containing one! Optionally, mix in some raw pumpkin seeds, sunflower seeds, or dry-roasted pistachios.

- ¾ cup kefir or whole milk yogurt
- 2 tablespoons crushed unsweetened pineapple
- 3 tablespoons shredded unsweetened coconut
- Sweetener (optional)

In a large glass, combine the kefir or yogurt, pineapple, coconut, and sweetener (if desired). Stir well.

PER SERVING: 247 calories, 8 g protein, 16 g carbohydrates, 17 g total fat, 13 g saturated fat, 3 g fiber, 90 mg sodium

APPLE PIE SMOOTHIE

Makes 1 serving

With all the flavors of a slice of freshly baked apple pie, this smoothie can be served as a stand-alone breakfast, as a delicious topping for vanilla ice cream, or as a simple dessert.

1 cup kefir or whole milk yogurt

2 tablespoons finely chopped apple

Sweetener equivalent to 2 tablespoons sugar

¼ teaspoon ground cinnamon

¼ teaspoon ground nutmeg

In a large glass, combine the kefir or yogurt, apple, sweetener, cinnamon, and nutmeg. Stir well.

PER SERVING: 162 calories, 9 g protein, 14 g carbohydrates, 8 g total fat, 5 g saturated fat, 1 g fiber, 113 mg sodium

CHOCOLATE-COCONUT SMOOTHIE

Makes 1 serving

If you love chocolate without coconut, just leave out the coconut. And the mint extract was added for you mint lovers, but it's optional. For extra decadence, add some mini dark chocolate chips.

1 cup kefir or whole milk yogurt

2 tablespoons unsweetened shredded coconut

2 teaspoons unsweetened cocoa powder

Sweetener equivalent to 2 tablespoons sugar

3 drops natural peppermint extract (optional)

In a large glass, combine the kefir or yogurt, coconut, cocoa, sweetener, and peppermint extract (if desired). Stir well.

PER SERVING: 238 calories, 10 g protein, 16 g carbohydrates, 16 g total fat, 11 g saturated fat, 3 g fiber, 117 mg sodium

QUICK MUFFINS

Quick muffins are single-serve muffins that you make in a mug or ramekin. Because they can be made in a microwave, the entire process takes about 5 minutes, perfect for a quick, on-the-run, healthy breakfast in the morning. If desired, quick muffins can also be baked in the oven using an ovenproof ramekin. Bake at 375°F for 25 minutes, or until a wooden pick inserted in the center comes out clean. And, as always, taste your batter before cooking to gauge sweetness and adjust if needed.

KID-FRIENDLY

APPLE-SPICE QUICK MUFFIN

PREP TIME: 5 MINUTES | **TOTAL TIME:** 5 MINUTES

Makes 1 muffin

This basic muffin can be made spicier by adding ⅛ teaspoon cloves, finely chopped apples, and more applesauce, particularly if you are not too concerned with carbohydrate exposure (such as with kids or serious athletes).

½ cup All-Purpose Baking Mix (page 19)

¼ teaspoon ground cinnamon

⅛ teaspoon ground nutmeg

Sweetener equivalent to 1 tablespoon sugar

Pinch of sea salt

1 egg

2 tablespoons unsweetened applesauce

1 tablespoon butter, melted

In a medium bowl, combine the baking mix, cinnamon, nutmeg, sweetener, and salt. Whisk in the egg. Add the applesauce and butter, and whisk thoroughly. Use a rubber spatula to scrape the mixture into a large mug or a 10-ounce ramekin.

Microwave on high power for 2 minutes, or until a wooden pick inserted in the center comes out clean. Allow to cool for 5 minutes.

PER MUFFIN: 506 calories, 19 g protein, 19 g carbohydrates, 43 g total fat, 11 g saturated fat, 10 g fiber, 644 mg sodium

TRIPLE-BERRY QUICK MUFFIN

PREP TIME: 5 MINUTES | **TOTAL TIME:** 5 MINUTES

Makes 1 muffin

These simple, quick muffins are packed with healthy ingredients: nuts, berries, and plenty of protein and good-for-you fats. For crunch, consider adding dry-roasted (unsalted) pistachios or cashew, walnut, or pecan fragments.

½ cup All-Purpose Baking Mix (page 19)

¼ teaspoon ground cinnamon

Sweetener equivalent to 1 tablespoon sugar

Pinch of sea salt

1 egg

2 tablespoons milk

1 tablespoon butter, melted

¼ cup frozen or fresh mixed berries

In a medium bowl, combine the baking mix, cinnamon, sweetener, and salt. Whisk in the egg. Add the milk, butter, and berries and whisk thoroughly. Use a rubber spatula to scrape the mixture into a large mug or a 10-ounce ramekin.

Microwave on high power for 2 minutes, or until a wooden pick inserted in the center comes out clean. (If using fresh berries, microwave for 1½ minutes.) Allow to cool for 5 minutes.

PER MUFFIN: 526 calories, 20 g protein, 21 g carbohydrates, 44 g total fat, 11 g saturated fat, 11 g fiber, 558 mg sodium

COCONUT-CHOCOLATE QUICK MUFFIN

PREP TIME: 5 MINUTES | **TOTAL TIME:** 5 MINUTES

Makes 1 muffin

If a richer, though higher in carbohydrate/sugar muffin is desired (such as for the kids), add a tablespoon of dark chocolate chips prior to microwaving or top with dark chocolate shavings after microwaving.

½ cup All-Purpose Baking Mix (page 19)

2 teaspoons unsweetened cocoa powder

1 tablespoon unsweetened shredded coconut

¼ teaspoon ground cinnamon

Sweetener equivalent to 2 tablespoons sugar

Pinch of sea salt

1 egg

2 tablespoons milk

1 tablespoon butter, melted

In a medium bowl, combine the baking mix, cocoa, coconut, cinnamon, sweetener, and salt. Whisk in the egg. Add the milk and butter and whisk thoroughly. Use a rubber spatula to scrape the mixture into a large mug or 10-ounce ramekin.

Microwave on high power for 2 minutes, or until a wooden pick inserted in the center comes out clean. Allow to cool for 5 minutes.

PER MUFFIN: 554 calories, 20 g protein, 19 g carbohydrates, 48 g total fat, 14 g saturated fat, 11 g fiber, 553 mg sodium

BLUEBERRY CHEESECAKE FRUIT CUPS

PREP TIME: 10 MINUTES | **TOTAL TIME:** 10 MINUTES

Makes 4 servings

Can anybody turn down blueberry cheesecake for breakfast?

Remember: In the wheat-free lifestyle, problem ingredients are replaced with healthy ingredients. This means that dishes like these simple Blueberry Cheesecake Fruit Cups can serve as a healthy breakfast.

1 cup heavy cream

8 ounces cream cheese, softened

Sweetener equivalent to ⅓ cup sugar, or to taste

½ teaspoon lemon extract

½ cup whole milk plain Greek yogurt

1 cup blueberries

½ cup chopped walnuts

In a chilled medium bowl, whip the cream with an electric mixer for 3 to 4 minutes, or until stiff peaks form. Set aside.

In another medium bowl using the same beaters, beat the cream cheese for 1 minute, or until creamy. Add the sweetener, lemon extract, and yogurt and beat for 1 minute, or just until blended. Gently fold in the whipped cream until well combined. Fold in the blueberries and walnuts.

Evenly divide into 4 parfait glasses or serving dishes. Serve immediately, or chill until firm, if desired.

PER SERVING: 531 calories, 12 g protein, 12 g carbohydrates, 51 g total fat, 25 g saturated fat, 2 g fiber, 200 mg sodium

BREAKFAST NUT MIX

PREP TIME: 10 MINUTES | **TOTAL TIME:** 20 MINUTES + COOLING TIME

Makes 9 cups

Here's your answer to breakfast cereal—but this cereal has *none* of the problems of the stuff that lines an entire aisle at your supermarket! Serve this nut mix with some coconut milk, almond milk, or dairy milk, cold or hot. Top with ¼ cup fresh, dried, or freeze-dried unsweetened pomegranate or other dried unsweetened berries per serving.

I make use of the modest fruit sugar in raisins. If you're serving the granola to your children and they prefer it sweeter, add just a bit of stevia or other sweetener. The use of raisins will allow you to minimize the use of sweetener.

¼ cup raisins	2 cups raw sunflower seeds
½ cup coconut milk	2 cups raw pumpkin seeds
2 tablespoons coconut oil, melted	1 cup raw chopped pecans
1 teaspoon vanilla extract	1 cup raw sliced almonds
½ teaspoon almond extract	2 cups unsweetened coconut flakes

Preheat the oven to 350°F.

In a food chopper or food processor, chop or pulse the raisins until reduced to a paste. Place in a small bowl and add the coconut milk and oil. Mix thoroughly. Add the vanilla and almond extract and stir to combine. Set aside.

In a large bowl, combine the sunflower seeds, pumpkin seeds, pecans, almonds, and coconut. Stir in the reserved raisin mixture until well mixed.

Spread on a large baking sheet and bake for 15 minutes, stirring once, or until lightly browned. Remove and allow to cool.

PER ½ CUP: 329 calories, 9 g protein, 11 g carbohydrates, 28 g total fat, 11 g saturated fat, 4 g fiber, 7 mg sodium

LIGHT MEALS
AND SIDE DISHES

CREAM OF MUSHROOM SOUP WITH CHIVES

PREP TIME: 10 MINUTES | **TOTAL TIME:** 30 MINUTES

Makes 8 servings

Wheat-free and dairy-free, this creamy mushroom soup makes a filling meal by itself or a substantial accompaniment to pork, chicken, or beef dishes.

If dairy avoidance is not an issue for you, the olive oil can be substituted with butter, and the coconut milk substituted with cream, half-and-half, or whole milk.

2 tablespoons extra-virgin olive oil

1 yellow onion, finely chopped

2 cloves garlic, minced

16 ounces baby bella, cremini, or button mushrooms, coarsely chopped

1 teaspoon sea salt, or to taste

½ teaspoon ground black pepper

3 cups chicken stock

1 can (14 ounces) coconut milk

2 tablespoons chopped fresh chives

In a large skillet over medium-high heat, heat the oil. Cook the onion for 3 minutes, or until soft. Add the garlic and cook for 1 minute. Add the mushrooms, salt, and pepper. Reduce the heat to medium, cover, and cook for 5 minutes, or until the mushrooms are softened.

Stir in the chicken stock and coconut milk. Bring to a slow boil and simmer for 3 minutes.

Ladle or pour the mixture into a blender and blend until smooth (in batches, if necessary). Serve topped with the chives.

PER SERVING: 181 calories, 5 g protein, 8 g carbohydrates, 15 g total fat, 10 g saturated fat, 2 g fiber, 338 mg sodium

CURRY CAULIFLOWER SOUP

PREP TIME: 5 MINUTES | **TOTAL TIME:** 30 MINUTES

Makes 4 servings

As with most dishes in our wheat-free world, this soup is deceptively filling. This rich, thick cauliflower soup, with the flavor of curry, will warm your insides and satisfy you served by itself or with finger sandwiches, biscuits, or a green salad.

2 tablespoons extra-virgin olive oil

1 large onion, halved and sliced

1 large head cauliflower, chopped

2 tablespoons curry powder

1 teaspoon ground cumin

¼ teaspoon sea salt

4 cups chicken stock, divided

1 cup heavy cream or canned coconut milk

In a large saucepan over medium-high heat, heat the oil. Add the onion and cauliflower and cook for 10 minutes, or until browned. Stir in the curry powder, cumin, and salt. Cook for 1 minute. Add 2 cups of the stock, and bring to a boil. Reduce the heat to medium and cook, covered, for 8 minutes, or until the cauliflower is very tender.

Ladle or pour the mixture into a blender and blend until smooth (in batches, if necessary). Return to the saucepan with the cream or coconut milk and the remaining 2 cups stock. Stir to combine. Cook for 5 minutes.

PER SERVING: 370 calories, 11 g protein, 19 g carbohydrates, 30 g total fat, 15 g saturated fat, 6 g fiber, 618 mg sodium

TOMATO AND FENNEL SOUP

PREP TIME: 5 MINUTES | **TOTAL TIME:** 25 MINUTES

Makes 4 servings

This simple soup recipe requires only a few minutes of preparation, but yields a tasty, filling accompaniment to any meat dish. Optionally, add chicken or pork by browning the meat first, then tossing it into the mix.

¼ cup extra-virgin olive oil

1 large yellow onion, thinly sliced

1 bulb fennel, halved, cored, and thinly sliced

2 cloves garlic, minced

2½ cups chicken stock

1 can (14.5 ounces) diced tomatoes

½ teaspoon sea salt

In a large skillet over medium-high heat, heat the oil. Cook the onion, fennel, and garlic for 10 minutes, or until very soft. (Reduce the heat to medium, if necessary, to keep the vegetables from overbrowning.)

Add the stock, tomatoes with their juice, and salt and bring to a boil. Reduce the heat to a simmer, cover, and cook for 10 minutes.

PER SERVING: 200 calories, 5 g protein, 14 g carbohydrates, 14 g total fat, 2 g saturated fat, 3 g fiber, 727 mg sodium

EGG DROP SOUP

PREP TIME: 5 MINUTES | **TOTAL TIME:** 10 MINUTES

Makes 4 servings

This Chinese restaurant favorite is healthy and simple to re-create, though minus the unhealthy thickeners often used. This basic recipe is easily modified by adding, for instance, a tablespoon of Sriracha sauce or some stir-fried vegetables.

4 cups chicken stock

1 teaspoon grated fresh ginger

1 teaspoon tamari or gluten-free soy sauce

¼ teaspoon sea salt

2 teaspoons coconut flour

2 eggs, whisked

3 scallions, sliced diagonally

In a large saucepan, bring the stock, ginger, tamari or soy sauce, and salt to a slow boil. Stir in the flour until dissolved. Turn off the heat. From approximately 8 to 10" above the soup, slowly drizzle in the eggs while stirring the soup slowly in a circular motion. Continue to stir for approximately 30 seconds after the eggs have been poured in.

Stir in the scallions and serve.

PER SERVING: 57 calories, 5 g protein, 3 g carbohydrates, 3 g total fat, 1 g saturated fat, 1 g fiber, 1,083 mg sodium

HAMBURGER SOUP

PREP TIME: 5 MINUTES | **TOTAL TIME:** 25 MINUTES

Makes 4 servings

This kid-pleaser is an easy tummy-filler, and also easy to adapt to personal taste. It can be topped with sour cream, grated Romano or Parmesan cheese, or another shredded cheese of your choosing.

2 tablespoons extra-virgin olive oil

1 yellow onion, finely chopped

2 carrots, sliced

1 green bell pepper, coarsely chopped

2 ribs celery, halved lengthwise and sliced

1 pound ground beef

1 teaspoon Italian Seasoning Mix (page 56)

¼ teaspoon sea salt

4 cups beef stock

In a large skillet over medium-high heat, heat the oil. Cook the onion, carrots, pepper, and celery, stirring occasionally, for 3 minutes, or until starting to soften. Add the beef and cook for 3 minutes, or until barely pink. Add the seasoning mix and salt and cook for 1 minute.

Pour in the stock and bring to a boil. Reduce the heat to medium and simmer for 10 minutes, or until the vegetables are softened.

PER SERVING: 407 calories, 26 g protein, 9 g carbohydrates, 30 g total fat, 10 g saturated fat, 2 g fiber, 644 mg sodium

NEW ORLEANS GUMBO

PREP TIME: 10 MINUTES | **TOTAL TIME:** 30 MINUTES

Makes 4 servings

It seems like everyone from Louisiana has a favorite recipe for gumbo. All involve various methods to thicken the roux. Here, for the sake of adhering to the 30-minute timeline, I use coconut flour rather than the traditional methods, a technique that shaves off about 15 or more minutes. This recipe can serve as the basis for any number of variations, such as substituting shrimp for the chicken.

2 tablespoons extra-virgin olive oil or coconut oil

1 pound andouille sausage, sliced

1 pound boneless, skinless chicken breasts, cut into cubes

3 cups chicken stock, divided

2–3 tablespoons coconut flour

1 large onion, finely chopped

2 garlic cloves, minced

1 large green bell pepper, chopped

1 teaspoon Cajun Seasoning Mix (page 58)

1 can (14.5 ounces) diced tomatoes

In a large skillet or saucepan over medium-high heat, heat the oil. Cook the sausage and chicken, stirring occasionally, for 7 minutes, or until lightly browned. Reduce the heat to medium. With a slotted spoon, transfer the sausage and chicken to a bowl, leaving the liquid in the skillet, and set aside.

Pour 1 cup of the chicken stock in the skillet or saucepan. Stir in the coconut flour, 1 tablespoon every 30 seconds, until the desired thickness is achieved.

Add the onion, garlic, pepper, and seasoning mix. Cook, stirring occasionally, for 3 minutes, or until the vegetables begin to soften.

Return the reserved sausage and chicken to the skillet or saucepan, along with the tomatoes with their juice and the remaining 2 cups chicken stock. Cover and cook for 8 minutes, or until the chicken is cooked through and the vegetables are softened.

PER SERVING: 500 calories, 50 g protein, 15 g carbohydrates, 27 g total fat, 8 g saturated fat, 4 g fiber, 1,540 mg sodium

CREAM OF CRAB SOUP

PREP TIME: 10 MINUTES | **TOTAL TIME:** 30 MINUTES

Makes 8 servings

Here's the creamiest of cream soups, thickened the good, old-fashioned way without cornstarch, wheat flour, or other thickeners.

1 tablespoon butter

2 shallots, minced

1 small red bell pepper, finely chopped

3 ounces cream cheese, cut into cubes

4 cups heavy cream

½ teaspoon sea salt

¼ teaspoon ground black pepper

1 pound backfin lump crabmeat

2 tablespoons sherry

1 teaspoon Cajun Seasoning Mix (page 58)

In a medium saucepan over medium heat, melt the butter. Cook the shallots and bell pepper for 5 minutes, or until tender. Add the cream cheese and stir for 1 minute, or until melted. Stir in the cream, salt, and black pepper. Heat until the mixture just begins to simmer (do not boil).

Reduce the heat to medium-low and simmer for 5 minutes, stirring frequently. Stir in the crabmeat, sherry, and seasoning mix and cook for 5 minutes, or until heated through.

PER SERVING: 534 calories, 17 g protein, 4 g carbohydrates, 50 g total fat, 31 g saturated fat, 0 g fiber, 415 mg sodium

NEW ENGLAND CLAM CHOWDER

PREP TIME: 10 MINUTES | **TOTAL TIME:** 30 MINUTES

Makes 4 servings

Here's how you make a New England Clam Chowder with no problem ingredients. Enjoy this heart-warming and delicious dish with some Pesto Breakfast Biscuits (page 77).

This clam chowder can be made using half-and-half or coconut milk. The non-dairy coconut version is surprisingly tasty and rich.

12 ounces bacon, cut into 1" pieces

1 onion, finely chopped

3 ribs celery, halved and sliced

2 cups half-and-half or canned coconut milk

2 teaspoons dried thyme

1 small head cauliflower, chopped into ½" pieces

¼ teaspoon sea salt

1 can (10 ounces) clams

In a large saucepan over medium-high heat, cook the bacon for 5 minutes, or until cooked through but not crispy. With tongs or a slotted spoon, remove the bacon, leaving the drippings, and place on a plate. Set aside.

Add the onion and celery and cook, stirring frequently, for 3 minutes, or until starting to soften. Stir in the half-and-half or coconut milk, thyme, cauliflower, and salt. Bring to a simmer. Reduce the heat to medium-low, cover, and simmer, stirring occasionally, for 15 minutes, or until the cauliflower is softened.

Add the reserved bacon and the clams with their juice. Cover and cook for 3 minutes, or until heated through.

PER SERVING: 616 calories, 27 g protein, 17 g carbohydrates, 50 g total fat, 21 g saturated fat, 3 g fiber, 1,143 mg sodium

TUNA-TOMATO MELTS

PREP TIME: 10 MINUTES | **TOTAL TIME:** 20 MINUTES

Makes 4 servings

While they can be eaten as lunch by themselves, or as a side dish with dinner, these Tuna-Tomato Melts also make a wonderful, healthy, and filling breakfast alternative.

2 cans (5 ounces each) wild-caught tuna, drained

½ cup Mayonnaise (page 40 or store-bought)

1 tablespoon Dijon mustard

1 rib celery, finely diced

2 scallions, thinly sliced

1 cup shredded Cheddar cheese, divided

4 large plum tomatoes, halved lengthwise

Preheat the oven to 375°F. Lightly grease a shallow 1½- or 2-quart baking dish.

In a medium bowl, with a fork or the back of a spoon, break up the tuna into small chunks. Add the mayonnaise, mustard, celery, scallions, and ½ cup of the cheese and mix until well blended.

Using a spoon, scoop out the flesh of each tomato half and discard. Fill each hollowed tomato half with the tuna mixture, mounding slightly, and place in the baking dish.

Bake for 8 minutes, or until hot. Remove from the oven and turn the oven to broil. While the broiler is heating, top each tomato half with 1 tablespoon of the remaining cheese. Broil for 2 minutes, or until the cheese is melted and bubbly.

PER SERVING: 323 calories, 22 g protein, 12 g carbohydrates, 21 g total fat, 8 g saturated fat, 1 g fiber, 715 mg sodium

EGGPLANT CAPRESE STACKS

PREP TIME: 15 MINUTES | **TOTAL TIME:** 30 MINUTES

Makes 4 servings

Eggplant, basil, and Parmesan and mozzarella cheeses combine to make a confident main dish all by itself or a bold side dish alongside a shirataki noodle or spaghetti squash "pasta" dish topped with marinara sauce.

1 eggplant, cut into eight ¼"-thick slices

¼ cup ground golden flaxseeds

½ cup finely grated Parmesan cheese, divided

½ teaspoon Italian Seasoning Mix (page 56)

½ teaspoon sea salt

1 egg, beaten

4 tablespoons olive oil, divided

2 tomatoes, each cut into four ½"-thick slices

16 large fresh basil leaves

8 ounces fresh mozzarella, cut into 4 equal slices

Lightly grease a baking sheet.

In a shallow bowl or dish, combine the flaxseeds, ¼ cup of the Parmesan, the seasoning mix, and salt. Place the egg in another shallow bowl or dish. Dip a slice of the eggplant into the egg until both sides are moistened. Dredge in the flaxseed mixture to coat. Place the breaded eggplant on a plate. Repeat until all the slices have been coated.

In a large skillet over medium heat, heat 2 tablespoons of the oil until hot. Cook the eggplant, covered, for 8 minutes, turning once, or until browned on both sides and tender when pierced with a fork. If needed, add 1 tablespoon of the remaining oil during cooking. Transfer to a plate lined with a paper towel.

Meanwhile, preheat the broiler. Place the tomato slices in a single layer on the baking sheet. Drizzle with the remaining 1 tablespoon oil and sprinkle each with ½ tablespoon of the remaining Parmesan. Broil for 4 minutes, or until lightly browned. Remove and set aside.

On 4 plates, place the 4 largest eggplant slices. Top each slice with a broiled Parmesan tomato, 2 basil leaves, and a mozzarella slice. Top with the remaining eggplant slices, a Parmesan tomato, and 2 basil leaves.

PER SERVING: 377 calories, 21 g protein, 13 g carbohydrates, 29 g total fat, 9 g saturated fat, 7 g fiber, 276 mg sodium

CRAB-STUFFED DEVILED EGGS

PREP TIME: 10 MINUTES | TOTAL TIME: 10 MINUTES

Makes 12

Here's a quick variation on standard deviled eggs made more interesting with the addition of crabmeat.

6 hard-cooked eggs, peeled and halved lengthwise

1 can (6 ounces) crabmeat, drained

¼ cup + 1 tablespoon Mayonnaise (page 40 or store-bought)

½ teaspoon celery salt

1 tablespoon chopped fresh parsley

Place the egg yolks in a medium bowl. Arrange the egg whites on a serving plate.

Using a fork, mash the egg yolks. Add the crabmeat, mayonnaise, and celery salt. Stir until well combined. Spoon the mixture evenly into the egg white halves.

Sprinkle the parsley over the top of each egg half.

PER EGG HALF: 91 calories, 6 g protein, 0 g carbohydrates, 8 g total fat, 2 g saturated fat, 0 g fiber, 124 mg sodium

WASABI DEVILED EGGS

PREP TIME: 10 MINUTES | **TOTAL TIME:** 10 MINUTES

Makes 12

Here's a unique and simple variation on the familiar deviled egg—an Asian version with the zing of wasabi.

6 hard-cooked eggs, peeled and halved lengthwise

3 tablespoons Mayonnaise (page 40 or store-bought)

1 teaspoon wasabi powder

½ teaspoon ground ginger

½ teaspoon rice vinegar

Place the egg yolks in a medium bowl. Arrange the egg whites on a serving plate.

Using a fork, mash the egg yolks. Add the mayonnaise, wasabi, ginger, and vinegar. Stir until well combined. Spoon or pipe the mixture evenly into the egg white halves.

PER EGG HALF: 64 calories, 3 g protein, 0 g carbohydrates, 5 g total fat, 1 g saturated fat, 0 g fiber, 54 mg sodium

ROAST BEEF SANDWICHES
WITH HORSERADISH MAYONNAISE

PREP TIME: 5 MINUTES | **TOTAL TIME:** 5 MINUTES

Makes 2 servings

Here is the traditional deli-style roast beef sandwich made with Sandwich Bread, slathered with a horseradish mayonnaise, and combined with cheese and red onion.

¼ cup Mayonnaise (page 40 or store-bought)

2 teaspoons prepared horseradish

4 slices Sandwich Bread (page 20)

4 ounces deli-sliced roast beef

2 ounces sliced Swiss, provolone, or Asiago cheese

¼ small red onion, very thinly sliced

In a small bowl, combine the mayonnaise and horseradish.

Spread 2 slices of bread with 1 tablespoon of the mayonnaise mixture each. Layer half of the roast beef, cheese, and onion on each slice of bread. Spread the remaining mayonnaise mixture on top. Top with the remaining 2 slices of bread. If desired, microwave on high power for 20 seconds to melt the cheese.

PER SERVING: 724 calories, 33 g protein, 14 g carbohydrates, 63 g total fat, 16 g saturated fat, 7 g fiber, 911 mg sodium

AVOCADO-HAM SANDWICHES

PREP TIME: 5 MINUTES | TOTAL TIME: 5 MINUTES

Makes 2 servings

This simple sandwich presents several possibilities for unique variations just by altering the topping. Add thinly sliced tomatoes or sprouts for other easy variations. For a change of pace, you can also replace the ham with other lunchmeat—wheat free, of course!

4 slices Basic Focaccia Flatbread (page 21) or Sandwich Bread (page 20)

1 avocado, halved, pitted, peeled, and sliced, or 4 tablespoons Guacamole (page 32)

½ small red onion, thinly sliced

4 ounces sliced ham

2–3 tablespoons Herbed Ranch Dressing (page 44), Creamy Tomato-Cilantro Dressing (page 47), or Spicy Hummus (page 33)

Top 2 slices of bread with the avocado, onion, and ham. Drizzle with your choice of dressing or hummus. Top with the remaining 2 bread slices.

PER SERVING: 728 calories, 33 g protein, 26 g carbohydrates, 59 g total fat, 8 g saturated fat, 15 g fiber, 1,201 mg sodium

MUFFULETTA SANDWICHES

PREP TIME: 5 MINUTES | **TOTAL TIME:** 5 MINUTES

Makes 4 servings

This traditional New Orleans sandwich, dripping with olive oil and chopped olives, comes in many different versions, each with enthusiastic followers. Besides not using wheat-based bread, I depart from the usual routine by using Asiago cheese for an extra-cheesy "kick."

Muffuletta is properly served on sesame seed–coated bread. So, if adhering to tradition is important to you, make your Basic Focaccia Flatbread with sesame seeds sprinkled on top.

4 slices Basic Focaccia Flatbread (page 21)

¼ cup muffuletta spread or tapenade

4 ounces sliced ham

2 ounces sliced pepperoni

2 ounces sliced mortadella

4 ounces sliced provolone cheese

2 ounces sliced Asiago cheese

Spread 2 slices of bread with the muffuletta spread or tapenade. Top evenly with the ham, pepperoni, mortadella, provolone, and Asiago. Top with the remaining 2 slices of bread. Carefully slice each sandwich in half.

PER SERVING: 619 calories, 32 g protein, 14 g carbohydrates, 50 g total fat, 14 g saturated fat, 7 g fiber, 1,766 mg sodium

KID-FRIENDLY

PROSCIUTTO-PROVOLONE FOCACCIA

PREP TIME: 5 MINUTES | TOTAL TIME: 10 MINUTES

Makes 4 servings

This unique sandwich provides a medley of Italian flavors: aged prosciutto, provolone, artichokes, and sun-dried tomatoes.

4 slices Basic Focaccia Flatbread (page 21) or Herbed Focaccia Flatbread (page 22)

2 cups baby spinach

2 ounces prosciutto

4 slices provolone cheese

4 canned artichoke hearts, sliced

2 tablespoons Sun-Dried Tomato Italian Dressing (page 50) or other Italian dressing

Preheat the oven to 350°F.

On a baking sheet, arrange the flatbread slices. Top evenly with the spinach, prosciutto, cheese, and artichokes. Bake for 3 minutes, or until the cheese is melted. Drizzle with the dressing.

PER SERVING: 471 calories, 24 g protein, 14 g carbohydrates, 38 g total fat, 9 g saturated fat, 7 g fiber, 1,147 mg sodium

PEPPERONI BREAD

PREP TIME: 10 MINUTES | TOTAL TIME: 30 MINUTES + COOLING TIME

Makes 8 servings

If you see the kids gobble this Pepperoni Bread down, don't be fooled: It just *looks* unhealthy! After all, this "bread" is really just made of ground nuts, coconut, cheese, eggs, and pepperoni. Serve this side dish alongside a shirataki or spaghetti squash pasta dish topped with Marinara Sauce (page 34), or just serve the bread and sauce without any pasta.

1 cup shredded mozzarella cheese, divided

2 cups All-Purpose Baking Mix (page 19)

2 tablespoons extra-virgin olive oil

2 eggs, lightly whisked

1 teaspoon Italian Seasoning Mix (page 56)

2 ounces pepperoni, thinly sliced

Preheat the oven to 350°F. Line a baking sheet with parchment paper.

In a food processor, pulse ½ cup of the cheese until it's a granular consistency. In a large bowl, combine the cheese with the baking mix. Stir in the oil and eggs until thoroughly mixed. The dough will be thick but moist.

With moistened hands, spread the dough onto the baking sheet and form into a 10" x 10" square about ½" thick. Sprinkle the seasoning mix over the dough. Arrange the pepperoni over the dough, followed by the remaining ½ cup cheese.

Using the parchment paper, carefully roll one end of the bread, like a jelly roll, until the dough is fully rolled. (It may crack initially, but the outer layer will be intact.) Bake for 20 minutes, or until lightly browned.

Allow to cool for 5 minutes before slicing.

PER SERVING: 284 calories, 13 g protein, 8 g carbohydrates, 24 g total fat, 4.5 g saturated fat, 5 g fiber, 364 mg sodium

ITALIAN SAUSAGE MEATBALLS WITH RED WINE SAUCE

PREP TIME: 10 MINUTES | **TOTAL TIME:** 30 MINUTES

Makes 4 servings

These meatballs can go anywhere conventional meatballs can go: alone as an hors d'oeuvre, on top of shirataki noodles, or by themselves as a casual main dish with a green salad or steamed green beans, kale, broccoli, or asparagus.

Any ground meat can be substituted for the Italian sausage.

1 pound ground Italian sausage

2 tablespoons ground golden flaxseeds

1 egg

½ teaspoon Italian Seasoning Mix (page 56)

¼ teaspoon sea salt

2 tablespoons extra-virgin olive oil or coconut oil

2 tablespoons tomato sauce

¼ cup dry red wine

In a large bowl, combine the sausage, flaxseeds, egg, seasoning mix, and salt and mix thoroughly. Form into 1½" balls.

In a large skillet over medium-high heat, heat the oil. Cook the meatballs for 2 minutes, turning to brown all sides. Reduce the heat to medium-low, cover, and cook for 12 minutes, stirring frequently, or until no longer pink.

With a slotted spoon, transfer the meatballs to a serving bowl.

In the same skillet over low heat, cook the tomato sauce and wine for 2 minutes, stirring to loosen any brown bits from the bottom of the skillet, or until heated through. Pour over meatballs.

PER SERVING: 503 calories, 19 g protein, 3 g carbohydrates, 45 g total fat, 14 g saturated fat, 1 g fiber, 986 mg sodium

OPEN-FACED CHICKEN CAPRESE FOCACCIA

PREP TIME: 5 MINUTES | **TOTAL TIME:** 20 MINUTES

Makes 4 servings

The flavors of fresh basil, mozzarella cheese, and tomato that make Caprese salads a perennial favorite combine to make a delightful and quick open-faced sandwich. Optionally, drizzle a few drops of balsamic vinegar over the top when adding the basil.

4 slices Basic Focaccia Flatbread (page 21)

2–3 tablespoons Italian Seasoning Mix (page 56)

½ teaspoon sea salt

2 boneless, skinless chicken breast halves

1 large tomato, cut into 4 slices

4 ounces mozzarella cheese, sliced

¼ cup torn fresh basil

Place the oven rack 6" from the heat source and preheat the oven to broil. Place the focaccia on a baking sheet. Set aside. Grease a baking pan.

In a large resealable plastic bag, combine the seasoning mix and salt. Add the chicken and shake to coat.

Place the chicken in the baking pan and broil for 12 minutes, turning once, or until a thermometer inserted in the thickest portion registers 165°F and the juices run clear. Let stand for 5 minutes. Cut into thin slices.

Divide the chicken, tomato, and cheese among the focaccia. Broil for 1 minute, or until the cheese is melted. Sprinkle the basil over the top of each.

PER SERVING: 490 calories, 37 g protein, 15 g carbohydrates, 33 g total fat, 7 g saturated fat, 8 g fiber, 982 mg sodium

BACON AND BALSAMIC CHICKEN WRAPS

PREP TIME: 5 MINUTES | **TOTAL TIME:** 15 MINUTES

Makes 4 servings

The combination of bacon and reduced balsamic vinegar adds a wonderful dimension of flavor to this chicken wrap. Add sliced tomatoes or Guacamole (page 32) for variation.

2 tablespoons extra-virgin olive oil

1 boneless, skinless chicken breast, cut into thin strips

4 slices thick-cut bacon

4 ounces portobello mushrooms, sliced

2 tablespoons balsamic vinegar

4 Flaxseed Wraps (page 26)

2 cups shredded romaine lettuce

In a large skillet over medium-high heat, heat the oil. Cook the chicken, bacon, and mushrooms for 8 minutes, or until the chicken is no longer pink, the bacon is cooked through, and the mushrooms are golden. With a slotted spoon, transfer the chicken and bacon to a plate and set aside.

Reduce the heat to low. Add the vinegar to the mushrooms in the skillet. Simmer, stirring, for 1 minute, or until the vinegar has reduced. Remove from the heat.

Lay the wraps on a work surface. Arrange the reserved chicken and bacon down the center of each wrap. Top with the lettuce and mushroom mixture. Roll up.

PER SERVING: 394 calories, 25 g protein, 12 g carbohydrates, 29 g total fat, 8 g saturated fat, 9 g fiber, 384 mg sodium

AVOCADO, BACON, AND EGG SANDWICHES

PREP TIME: 5 MINUTES | TOTAL TIME: 20 MINUTES

Makes 2 servings

The combination of Cajun spices and bacon is surprisingly mouthwatering, especially along with the cool, creamy feel of fresh avocado. Don't let the small size of these sandwiches fool you: They are wonderfully filling!

4 slices thick-cut bacon

2 eggs

4 slices Sandwich Bread (page 20)

¼ cup Spicy Cajun Mayo (page 42)

1 avocado, halved, pitted, peeled, and sliced

In a large skillet over medium heat, cook the bacon until cooked through. Remove and set aside. Break the eggs into the skillet, keeping them separate. Break the yolks open and cook until firm. Optionally, use a circular egg mold to maintain a "clean" egg shape.

Spread 2 of the bread slices with 1 tablespoon of the mayo. Layer each with the reserved bacon, 1 egg, and the avocado. Spread the remaining mayonnaise on top, and then top with the remaining 2 bread slices.

PER SERVING: 722 calories, 27 g protein, 19 g carbohydrates, 63 g total fat, 14 g saturated fat, 12 g fiber, 855 mg sodium

TEX-MEX EGG SALAD WRAPS

PREP TIME: 5 MINUTES | **TOTAL TIME:** 5 MINUTES

Makes 4 servings

Taco seasoning and Dijon mustard liven up old-fashioned egg salad to make a delicious wrap. Serve with one of the cream soups in this cookbook, such as Cream of Mushroom Soup with Chives (page 92), and you will be filled to bursting!

6 hard-cooked eggs, peeled and chopped

½ cup Mayonnaise (page 40 or store-bought)

1 tablespoon Dijon mustard or 2 teaspoons mustard powder

2 teaspoons Taco Seasoning Mix (page 57)

1 small onion, finely chopped

1 small tomato, finely chopped

4 Flaxseed Wraps (page 26)

2 cups Boston lettuce, salad greens, spinach, or arugula

In a large bowl, combine the eggs, mayonnaise, mustard, seasoning mix, onion, and tomato. Mix thoroughly.

Place the wraps on a work surface. Divide the egg salad among the wraps, spreading it down the center of each wrap. Top with the greens. Roll up.

PER SERVING: 580 calories, 23 g protein, 16 g carbohydrates, 50 g total fat, 12 g saturated fat, 9 g fiber, 460 mg sodium

HOT CAPRESE SANDWICHES

PREP TIME: 5 MINUTES | **TOTAL TIME:** 5 MINUTES

Makes 2 servings

If you love a simple but elegant Caprese salad, you'll love this equally simple and elegant sandwich based on the same theme!

Use ripe, juicy tomatoes, preferably beefsteak or any heirloom varieties you can find (or grow!).

4 slices Basic Focaccia Flatbread (page 21)

2 ounces sliced mozzarella cheese

2 medium tomatoes, sliced

12 medium to large fresh basil leaves, sliced lengthwise

3–4 teaspoons Spicy Italian Dressing (page 49)

Place 1 slice of flatbread on a plate and layer with the cheese and tomatoes. Scatter the basil over each. Drizzle with the dressing. Top with another slice of bread.

One at a time, microwave on high power for 30 to 60 seconds to melt the cheese. Or heat in a 325°F oven for 3 to 4 minutes, or until the cheese is melted.

PER SERVING: 728 calories, 30 g protein, 26 g carbohydrates, 60 g total fat, 10 g saturated fat, 14 g fiber, 1,031 mg sodium

BALSAMIC MUSHROOM WRAPS

PREP TIME: 5 MINUTES | **TOTAL TIME:** 15 MINUTES

Makes 4 servings

Mushrooms—which are rich in potassium, niacin, trace minerals, soluble fiber, and unique phytochemicals—are unsung heroes of nutrition, so you can never get too much of them! They are increasingly being recognized as providing unique anti-inflammatory, immune-enhancing, even cancer-protective effects.

Another variation on this basic theme: Use large portobello mushrooms, slice them, and grill. Add the grilled portobello slices to the wraps before rolling.

2 tablespoons olive oil

1 small onion, finely chopped

16 ounces sliced portobello or button mushrooms

1 medium green bell pepper, sliced

1 clove garlic, minced

2 tablespoons balsamic vinegar

½ teaspoon sea salt

4 Flaxseed Wraps (page 26)

2 cups baby spinach, arugula, or lettuce

In a large skillet over medium heat, heat the oil. Cook the onion, mushrooms, and pepper for 2 minutes, stirring frequently. Add the garlic and cook for 1 minute. Add the vinegar and salt. Cook for 3 minutes, or until the vinegar has nearly evaporated.

Place the wraps on a work surface. Spread the mushroom mixture down the center of each wrap. Top with the greens. Roll up.

PER SERVING: 345 calories, 16 g protein, 19 g carbohydrates, 26 g total fat, 7 g saturated fat, 11 g fiber, 450 mg sodium

PEPPERONI PIZZA WRAPS

PREP TIME: 5 MINUTES | **TOTAL TIME:** 10 MINUTES

Makes 4 servings

This wrap is almost *too* quick and easy! As with many dishes in our world minus wheat, don't let the modest size fool you: These simple wraps are deceptively filling. As with conventional pizza, this basic recipe can be readily modified: Add sautéed onions and green bell peppers; replace the pepperoni with salami, sausage, or ground hamburger; add provolone, Parmesan, or goat cheese.

4 Flaxseed Wraps (page 26)

½ cup pizza sauce or tomato sauce

2 ounces pepperoni, sliced

8 ounces mozzarella cheese, shredded or sliced

Place each wrap on a plate. Spread the pizza sauce or tomato sauce down the center of each wrap. Top with the pepperoni and sprinkle with cheese.

One at a time, microwave on high power for 30 to 60 seconds or broil for 30 to 60 seconds in the oven to melt the cheese. Roll up.

PER SERVING: 553 calories, 28 g protein, 14 g carbohydrates, 44 g total fat, 22 g saturated fat, 7 g fiber, 1,178 mg sodium

LOX WRAPS

PREP TIME: 5 MINUTES | **TOTAL TIME:** 5 MINUTES

Makes 4 servings

Lox and cream cheese are a simple dietary pleasure, but, of course, the bagels for this treat are forbidden in our wheat-free lifestyle. So here's a replacement version of the familiar lox and bagels that uses wheat-free tortillas but keeps the comforting flavors of cream cheese, salmon, and chives.

4 Tortillas (page 29)

4 ounces cream cheese, at room temperature

4 ounces lox

2 tablespoons capers, drained

2 tablespoons finely chopped fresh chives

Place the tortillas on a work surface. Spread the cream cheese in a thin layer over each tortilla. Top evenly with the lox. Arrange the capers down the center of each. Sprinkle the chives over each tortilla. Roll up.

PER SERVING: 293 calories, 16 g protein, 10 g carbohydrates, 24 g total fat, 7 g saturated fat, 8 g fiber, 963 mg sodium

TUNA-SPINACH BURGERS

PREP TIME: 15 MINUTES | **TOTAL TIME:** 25 MINUTES

Makes 4 servings

These healthy Tuna-Spinach Burgers, served as is or between two slices of Sandwich Bread (page 20) or Basic Focaccia Flatbread (page 21), can be varied by simply choosing among the different seasoning mixes.

3 tablespoons extra-virgin olive oil, divided

1 package (6 ounces) fresh baby spinach

2 cans (5 ounces each) wild-caught tuna, drained

½ small red bell pepper, finely chopped

1 tablespoon Dijon mustard

2 tablespoons Mayonnaise (page 40 or store-bought)

1 teaspoon seafood seasoning or seasoning mix of choice (pages 55–59)

1 egg

⅓ cup finely grated Parmesan cheese

¼ cup chickpea flour

In a large skillet over medium-high heat, heat 1 tablespoon of the oil until hot. Cook the spinach, stirring frequently, for 2 minutes, or just until wilted. Place in a mesh colander and press the excess liquid from the spinach. Coarsely chop.

In a medium bowl, with a fork or the back of a spoon, break the tuna up into small pieces. Add the chopped spinach, pepper, mustard, mayonnaise, seasoning mix, and egg. Mix together until well combined. Stir in the cheese and chickpea flour and mix well. Shape the mixture into 4 burgers, about 3½" in diameter.

In the same skillet over medium heat, heat the remaining 2 tablespoons oil until hot. Cook the burgers for 6 minutes, turning once, or until golden brown and heated through.

PER SERVING: 365 calories, 27 g protein, 10 g carbohydrates, 24 g total fat, 4 g saturated fat, 3 g fiber, 798 mg sodium

CREAM OF MUSHROOM SOUP WITH CHIVES | 92

PEPPERONI BREAD | 108

ZUCCHINI CAKES

PREP TIME: 10 MINUTES | **TOTAL TIME:** 20 MINUTES

Makes 4 servings

There are a number of different ways to enjoy these Italian-seasoned Zucchini Cakes. I like serving them topped with Marinara Sauce (page 34) as a side dish for dinner or topped with a fried or poached egg for breakfast. They can also be broken up into pieces to make an interesting topping to a salad, replacing the croutons, served with Spicy Italian Dressing (page 49).

1 zucchini, grated

1 egg, slightly beaten

2 teaspoons Italian Seasoning Mix (page 56)

½ cup shredded mozzarella cheese

¼ cup grated Parmesan cheese

¼ cup ground golden flaxseeds

2 tablespoons olive oil

Place the zucchini in the center of a clean kitchen towel or paper towels and wring or press out excess moisture.

In a medium bowl, combine the zucchini, egg, seasoning mix, and mozzarella. Add the Parmesan and flaxseeds and stir to combine thoroughly. Divide the batter into 4 equal portions and form into 4 cakes, ½" thick.

In a large skillet over medium-high heat, heat the oil until hot. Cook the cakes for 7 minutes, turning once, or until both sides are golden brown. Transfer to a plate lined with paper towels. Serve immediately.

PER SERVING: 192 calories, 10 g protein, 5 g carbohydrates, 16 g total fat, 4 g saturated fat, 3 g fiber, 235 mg sodium

ALMOND BUTTER AND JAM SANDWICH

PREP TIME: 5 MINUTES | **TOTAL TIME:** 5 MINUTES

Makes 1 serving

This is a more sophisticated adult version of the old PB & J sandwich! Almond butter replaces the peanut butter, but you can also use hazelnut butter, sunflower seed butter, or whatever other nut or seed butter strikes your fancy. Likewise, you can alter the basic recipe provided for Plum-Chia Jam to use your choice of fruit.

2 slices Sandwich Bread (page 20)

1–2 tablespoons almond butter

1 tablespoon Plum-Chia Jam (page 51) or other no-sugar-added preserves

On 1 slice of bread, spread the almond butter. Top with the jam or preserves and the remaining slice of bread.

PER SERVING: 456 calories, 17 g protein, 18 g carbohydrates, 39 g total fat, 8 g saturated fat, 9 g fiber, 499 mg sodium

ARTICHOKES, PANCETTA, AND KALE WITH SHAVED PARMESAN

PREP TIME: 5 MINUTES | TOTAL TIME: 15 MINUTES

Makes 6 servings

The taste contrasts of the pancetta, artichokes, kale, and Parmesan cheese make this dish a delight for the palate. While it can ably serve as a side dish alongside a wheat-free pasta dish or any meat, it can also make a healthy and filling stand-alone breakfast or lunch. For breakfast, top with a fried or poached egg.

If you don't have any premade Italian Seasoning Mix on hand, simply substitute 1 table-spoon dried oregano and 1 teaspoon dried rosemary.

2 tablespoons extra-virgin olive oil

4 ounces pancetta, sliced into 1" pieces

1 onion, finely chopped

2 cloves garlic, minced

1 teaspoon Italian Seasoning Mix (page 56)

8 ounces chopped frozen, thawed, kale

1 jar or can (12-14 ounces) quartered artichokes, drained

½ cup shaved Parmesan cheese

In a large skillet over medium-high heat, heat the oil. Cook the pancetta, onion, garlic, and Italian seasoning mix for 5 minutes, or until the pancetta is cooked through. If desired, drain off any excess oil.

Stir in the kale and artichokes. Reduce the heat to medium, cover, and cook for 5 minutes, or until the kale is wilted. Top with the cheese.

PER SERVING: 232 calories, 14 g protein, 13 g carbohydrates, 15 g total fat, 4 g saturated fat, 2 g fiber, 1,336 mg sodium

BRUSSELS SPROUTS GRATIN

PREP TIME: 5 MINUTES | **TOTAL TIME:** 30 MINUTES

Makes 4 servings

If you are new to the versatility of Brussels sprouts, let this dish get you acquainted! This is just one of the many ways to enjoy them—this time in a gratin dish.

As with all 30-minute meal dishes, don't let the butter and cheese fool you: Minus wheat and other unhealthy ingredients, this dish easily fits into a slimming and healthy lifestyle.

I like serving this with lighter proteins, such as white fish or chicken.

1 pound fresh Brussels sprouts, halved	¼ cup + 3 tablespoons shredded Parmesan cheese
1 cup water	¼ teaspoon sea salt
3 tablespoons butter, divided	¼ teaspoon ground black pepper
¼ cup almond meal/flour	½ cup heavy cream

Preheat the oven to 400°F. Lightly grease a 2-quart baking dish.

In a microwaveable bowl, place the Brussels sprouts and water. Cover and microwave on high power for 5 minutes. Drain well and toss the Brussels sprouts with 1 tablespoon of the butter.

Meanwhile, in a small bowl, combine the almond meal/flour, ¼ cup of the cheese, the salt, and pepper. Using a pastry blender or 2 forks, cut the remaining 2 tablespoons butter into the flour mixture until crumbly.

Arrange the Brussels sprouts in the bottom of the baking dish. Pour the cream over the Brussels sprouts and sprinkle evenly with the crumb topping. Scatter the remaining 3 tablespoons cheese over the crumb topping.

Bake for 20 minutes, or until golden brown and bubbling.

PER SERVING: 310 calories, 10 g protein, 13 g carbohydrates, 26 g total fat, 14 g saturated fat, 5 g fiber, 365 mg sodium

BUTTERED CABBAGE

PREP TIME: 5 MINUTES | **TOTAL TIME:** 10 MINUTES

Makes 4 servings

Although ultra-simple, I include this Buttered Cabbage recipe because it both comfortably accompanies many of the main dishes in this cookbook and can also serve as the basis for a variety of interesting side dishes. For instance, start with bacon, pancetta, or sausage before adding the cabbage; add Moroccan or Italian Seasoning Mix (pages 55 and 56) along with the salt and pepper; or replace the water with beef or chicken broth.

1 tablespoon extra-virgin olive oil	2 tablespoons butter
1 bag (16 ounces) shredded cabbage or coleslaw mix	¼ teaspoon sea salt
2 tablespoons water	¼ teaspoon ground black pepper

In a medium skillet or wok over medium-high heat, heat the oil until hot. Cook the cabbage, stirring constantly, for 3 minutes, or until it begins to soften. Add the water and continue to cook, stirring frequently, for 2 minutes, or until the cabbage is tender-crisp (or desired tenderness) and the water has evaporated. Add the butter and toss to coat. Season with the salt and pepper.

PER SERVING: 111 calories, 2 g protein, 7 g carbohydrates, 9 g total fat, 4 g saturated fat, 3 g fiber, 170 mg sodium

CAJUN KALE

PREP TIME: 5 MINUTES | TOTAL TIME: 30 MINUTES

Makes 4 servings

Using andouille sausage introduces the heady spices of Cajun cooking to the earthy greenness of kale. If you like a bit more tang, add an extra tablespoon of vinegar.

This simple recipe is also easily converted to Cajun Kale Soup by increasing the chicken stock to 2 cups, leaving out the vinegar, and seasoning with sea salt to taste.

2 tablespoons extra-virgin olive oil, divided

1 andouille smoked sausage link (3 ounces), diced

1 clove garlic, minced

1 bag (16 ounces) frozen kale greens, thawed

½ cup chicken stock

¼ teaspoon red-pepper flakes (optional)

1 tablespoon apple cider vinegar

In a medium saucepan or wok over medium heat, heat 1 tablespoon of the oil until hot. Cook the sausage for 4 minutes, or until lightly browned. Add the garlic and cook for 1 minute, stirring frequently. Transfer to a small plate and set aside.

In the same saucepan or wok, heat the remaining 1 tablespoon oil. Cook the kale, stirring constantly, for 2 minutes, or until coated with the oil and sizzling. Add the stock, cover, and cook, stirring occasionally, for 10 minutes, or until the kale is tender. Uncover and stir in the pepper flakes (if desired), vinegar, the reserved sausage and garlic, and the collected juices. Cook for 5 minutes, or until the liquid has nearly evaporated.

PER SERVING: 143 calories, 7 g protein, 7 g carbohydrates, 11 g total fat, 2 g saturated fat, 2 g fiber, 225 mg sodium

HERBES DE PROVENCE MUSHROOMS

PREP TIME: 5 MINUTES | **TOTAL TIME:** 15 MINUTES

Makes 4 servings

These ultrasimple spicy mushrooms burst with the flavors of the Herbes de Provence. They make an interesting and healthy accompaniment to steak or pork. They also make a tasty addition to a Mediterranean salad.

8 ounces cremini (or baby bella) mushrooms

2 tablespoons extra-virgin olive oil

1 teaspoon Herbes de Provence (page 59)

Preheat the oven to 350°F.

In a medium bowl, toss the mushrooms with the oil. Sprinkle with the Herbes de Provence and stir to coat evenly.

Place the mushrooms on a baking sheet. Bake for 10 minutes, tossing twice, or until browned.

PER SERVING: 77 calories, 1 g protein, 3 g carbohydrates, 7 g total fat, 1 g saturated fat, 1 g fiber, 4 mg sodium

ITALIAN MARINATED MUSHROOMS

PREP TIME: 5 MINUTES | **TOTAL TIME:** 20 MINUTES

Makes 4 servings

Super-duper quick and easy, these marinated mushrooms can be served as an appetizer or a side dish with steak, salmon, or baked chicken. Quick variations can be made by adding one or more finely chopped fresh herbs, such as oregano or marjoram.

2 tablespoons extra-virgin olive oil

16 ounces button or cremini mushrooms, stems removed

½ cup Spicy Italian Dressing (page 49)

In a large skillet over medium heat, heat the oil. Cook the mushrooms, stirring occasionally, covered, for 10 minutes, or until softened. Add the dressing and simmer for 3 minutes, or until the dressing is reduced by half.

PER SERVING: 260 calories, 3 g protein, 5 g carbohydrates, 26 g total fat, 4 g saturated fat, 1 g fiber, 105 mg sodium

CRAB-STUFFED PORTOBELLOS

PREP TIME: 15 MINUTES | **TOTAL TIME:** 30 MINUTES

Makes 6 servings

Crab plus cream cheese plus portobello mushrooms make a delicious, healthy, and surprisingly filling appetizer. I replace the usual bread crumbs with grated Parmesan cheese for a bit of crunch that also browns nicely in the oven.

1 **package (10 ounces) frozen chopped spinach, thawed and squeezed dry**

1 **can (6 ounces) crabmeat, drained**

8 **ounces cream cheese, softened**

1 **shallot, minced**

½ **teaspoon dried dillweed**

½ **teaspoon sea salt**

2 **tablespoons grated Parmesan cheese, divided**

12 **portobello mushrooms, approximately 3–4" diameter**

Preheat the oven to 400°F.

In a medium bowl, combine the spinach, crabmeat, cream cheese, shallot, dillweed, salt, and 1 tablespoon of the cheese.

Remove and discard the mushroom stems. Spoon the crab mixture into the stem side of the mushrooms and arrange on a baking sheet. Sprinkle the remaining 1 tablespoon cheese over the tops.

Bake for 15 minutes, or until the tops are golden and the mushrooms begin to release their juices.

PER SERVING: 227 calories, 12 g protein, 12 g carbohydrates, 14 g total fat, 8 g saturated fat, 3 g fiber, 446 mg sodium

SPINACH GRATIN

PREP TIME: 10 MINUTES | TOTAL TIME: 25 MINUTES

Makes 4 servings

This extra-cheesy spinach is a great way to get the kids (husbands included) to eat their spinach! Oozing with the smooth creaminess of a combination of heavy cream, cream cheese, butter, and melted Parmesan cheese, this dish is sure to get requests for seconds!

1 tablespoon extra-virgin olive oil

1 pound fresh baby spinach

1 tablespoon butter

2 tablespoons cream cheese

6 tablespoons heavy cream

½ cup shredded Parmesan cheese, divided

¼ teaspoon sea salt

¼ teaspoon ground black pepper

¼ cup almond meal/flour

Place an oven rack in the middle of the oven and preheat the broiler. Lightly grease a 1½-quart baking dish.

In a large skillet over medium heat, heat the oil until hot. Cook the spinach, tossing occasionally with tongs, for 4 minutes, or just until wilted. Push the spinach toward the sides of the skillet. Add the butter, cream cheese, and cream to the center of the skillet and stir for 2 minutes, or until melted and hot. Add ¼ cup of the Parmesan, the salt, and pepper. Stir the spinach and sauce together. Pour into the baking dish.

In a small bowl, combine the almond meal/flour and the remaining ¼ cup Parmesan. Sprinkle evenly over the spinach mixture.

Broil for 3 minutes, or until the topping is browned and the spinach is bubbly.

PER SERVING: 277 calories, 6 g protein, 14 g carbohydrates, 24 g total fat, 11 g saturated fat, 6 g fiber, 338 mg sodium

ANGEL HAIR SQUASH

PREP TIME: 10 MINUTES | **TOTAL TIME:** 15 MINUTES

Makes 4 servings

The first time I heard someone suggest the use of squash as a noodle replacement, I was skeptical. But once you give it a try, you will be pleasantly surprised at how wonderfully this healthy substitute takes the place of wheat pasta (or other unhealthy replacements), with *none* of the adverse health potential.

5 yellow summer squash	1 tablespoon butter
1 tablespoon extra-virgin olive oil	¼ teaspoon sea salt

Using a julienne vegetable slicer, mandoline, or spiral slicer, cut the squash into matchsticks. (You should have 4 cups). In a large skillet over medium-high heat, heat the oil until hot. Cook the squash, stirring frequently, for 2 to 3 minutes, or just until it begins to wilt and softens slightly (do not overcook). Stir in the butter until melted and season with the salt.

PER SERVING: 96 calories, 3 g protein, 8 g carbohydrates, 7 g total fat, 2 g saturated fat, 3 g fiber, 129 mg sodium

ZUCCHINI NOODLES

PREP TIME: 5 MINUTES | **TOTAL TIME:** 10 MINUTES

Makes 4 servings

Zucchini makes an excellent noodle replacement. It really helps to have one of the handy spiral slicers, such as a Spirelli or Spiralizer, or a julienne vegetable slicer, so converting zucchini into noodles is a snap. You can still do quite well by carefully cutting your zucchini with a sharp knife, veggie peeler, or mandoline.

½ teaspoon sea salt   2 pounds zucchini

In a medium saucepan, bring 2 quarts of water and the salt to a boil. Meanwhile, using a vegetable peeler or mandoline, cut the zucchini into long, thin, wide ribbon strips. (You should have 4 cups.) Add the ribbons to the water, reduce the heat to maintain a slow boil, and cook for 2 minutes, or until the zucchini is soft and flexible. Drain in a colander and serve with your choice of sauce.

PER SERVING: 39 calories, 3 g protein, 7 g carbohydrates, 1 g total fat, 0 g saturated fat, 2 g fiber, 94 mg sodium

Note: This recipe can also be made in a skillet. In a large nonstick skillet over medium-high heat, heat 2 tablespoons olive oil until hot. Cook the zucchini ribbons, stirring frequently, for 3 to 4 minutes, or until al dente (do not overcook). Add 1 tablespoon butter and toss with the zucchini to melt. Season with salt to taste.

ROASTED ZUCCHINI, SQUASH, AND TOMATO MEDLEY

PREP TIME: 10 MINUTES | **TOTAL TIME:** 30 MINUTES

Makes 4 servings

This colorful medley of vegetables is one of those recipes that can also serve as a vegetarian main dish, or serve it with your choice of baked chicken, fish, or pork.

1½ tablespoons olive oil

1 tablespoon red wine vinegar

½ teaspoon Italian Seasoning Mix (page 56)

½ teaspoon sea salt

2 yellow summer squash, sliced in ¼"-thick half-moon slices

1 zucchini, sliced in ¼"-thick half-moon slices

1 pint grape tomatoes, halved

⅓ cup finely shaved Parmesan cheese

Place an oven rack in the lower half of the oven and preheat the oven to 425°F.

In a large bowl, stir together the oil, vinegar, seasoning mix, and salt. Add the squash, zucchini, and tomatoes and toss to coat. Spread the vegetables in a single layer on a large baking sheet.

Bake for 20 minutes, stirring once, or until the vegetables are browned. Sprinkle with the cheese.

PER SERVING: 129 calories, 5 g protein, 11 g carbohydrates, 8 g total fat, 2 g saturated fat, 2 g fiber, 337 mg sodium

CURRIED "RICE"

PREP TIME: 5 MINUTES | **TOTAL TIME:** 15 MINUTES

Makes 4 servings

If you like the flavor of curry, you will love this simple Curried "Rice" that uses the ever-versatile cauliflower as a grain-free replacement. For added spiciness, add a teaspoon of the Moroccan Seasoning Mix (page 48).

1 small head cauliflower, broken into large pieces

2 tablespoons extra-virgin olive oil

1 onion, finely chopped

1 garlic clove, minced

1–2 teaspoons curry powder

½ teaspoon sea salt

Using a food processor with a shredding disk attachment or the largest holes of a box grater, shred the cauliflower. Place in a microwaveable bowl. Cover and microwave on high power for 4 minutes, stirring once, or until desired doneness.

Meanwhile, in a large skillet over medium heat, heat the oil. Cook the onion for 3 minutes, or until it begins to soften. Add the garlic and curry powder and cook for 1 minute, or until the curry is incorporated.

Add the steamed cauliflower and salt and stir to combine and heat through.

PER SERVING: 93 calories, 2 g protein, 6 g carbohydrates, 7 g total fat, 1 g saturated fat, 2 g fiber, 218 mg sodium

PORK FRIED "RICE"

PREP TIME: 10 MINUTES | **TOTAL TIME:** 20 MINUTES

Makes 6 servings

Don't you love the pork fried rice you get at your local Chinese restaurant? Here it is, re-created with healthy ingredients but without MSG, wheat, cornstarch, or rice.

Chicken, beef, and shrimp or other shellfish can readily serve as substitutes for the pork.

1 head cauliflower, broken into large pieces	2 eggs, whisked
2 tablespoons coconut oil, divided	½ pound pork tenderloin, cut into ½" cubes
4 scallions, sliced	¼ cup tamari or gluten-free soy sauce
2 cloves garlic, minced	

Using a food processor with a shredding disk attachment or the largest holes of a box grater, shred the cauliflower. Place in a microwaveable bowl. Cover and microwave on high power for 4 minutes, stirring once, or until desired doneness.

Meanwhile, in a wok or large skillet over medium-high heat, heat 1 tablespoon of the oil until hot. Cook the scallions and garlic for 2 minutes. Add the eggs and stir continuously until cooked through and lightly browned. Remove the egg mixture to a bowl and set aside.

Reduce the heat to medium. Add the remaining 1 tablespoon oil to the wok or skillet. Cook the pork, stirring frequently, for 5 minutes, or until no longer pink. Stir in the tamari or soy sauce, steamed cauliflower, and the reserved egg mixture. Cook, stirring, for 2 minutes, or until heated through.

PER SERVING: 141 calories, 13 g protein, 6 g carbohydrates, 7 g total fat, 5 g saturated fat, 2 g fiber, 702 mg sodium

MAIN DISHES

STEAK BÉARNAISE

PREP TIME: 5 MINUTES | **TOTAL TIME:** 15 MINUTES

Makes 4 servings

A French classic makes an appearance in the wheat-free lifestyle! Thick, rich, and buttery béarnaise sauce transforms an ordinary steak into an event.

To save time, I've streamlined the classic method for making béarnaise—it's so simple, you can make it while the steaks are cooking.

4 filets mignons or strip steaks (6 ounces each)

2 tablespoons olive oil

¼ teaspoon sea salt

¼ teaspoon ground black pepper

1 tablespoon lemon juice

2 teaspoons white wine vinegar

1 shallot, minced

2 egg yolks

2 tablespoons chopped fresh tarragon, divided

½ cup butter, melted

Pat both sides of the steaks dry using paper towels. Brush both sides with the oil and season with the salt and pepper.

Heat a well-seasoned indoor grill pan over medium-high heat until hot. Cook the steaks for 6 minutes, turning once, or until a thermometer inserted in the center registers 145°F for medium-rare. Transfer steaks to a platter.

Meanwhile, in a blender, combine the lemon juice, vinegar, shallot, egg yolks, and 1 tablespoon of the tarragon. Blend for 30 seconds, or until creamy. With the blender running, pour the melted butter in a slow, steady stream into the yolk mixture, then continue to blend for 30 seconds. Remove to a serving vessel and stir in the remaining 1 tablespoon tarragon.

Top steaks with the béarnaise sauce or serve on the side.

PER SERVING: 567 calories, 40 g protein, 1 g carbohydrates, 44 g total fat, 21 g saturated fat, 0 g fiber, 403 mg sodium

GINGER-SESAME PEPPER STEAK

PREP TIME: 15 MINUTES | **TOTAL TIME:** 25 MINUTES

Makes 4 servings

This simple stir-fried steak combined with the Asian flavors of ginger and sesame can make a substantial stand-alone main dish or can be served on top of shirataki noodles or "riced" cauliflower.

1 pound thin-sliced top sirloin steak (about ½" thick)

2 tablespoons coconut oil, divided

1 green bell pepper, cut into ¼" strips

1 red or yellow bell pepper, cut into ¼" strips

1 sweet onion, thinly sliced lengthwise

2 cloves garlic, minced

1 tablespoon grated fresh ginger

2 tablespoons tamari or gluten-free soy sauce

2 teaspoons sesame oil

Slice the steak crosswise against the grain into ¼"-wide strips.

In a wok or large skillet over high heat, heat 1 tablespoon of the coconut oil until hot. Stir-fry the peppers and onion for 3 minutes, or until tender-crisp. Transfer to a plate and set aside.

In the same wok or skillet, heat the remaining 1 tablespoon coconut oil until hot. Cook the steak strips for 1 minute, stirring constantly. Add the garlic and ginger and stir-fry for 2 minutes, or until the steak is browned. Stir in the tamari or soy sauce and sesame oil. Return the reserved peppers and onion to the wok and cook for 1 minute, tossing, or until hot.

PER SERVING: 270 calories, 27 g protein, 7 g carbohydrates, 15 g total fat, 8 g saturated fat, 2 g fiber, 540 mg sodium

BEEF STROGANOFF

PREP TIME: 10 MINUTES | **TOTAL TIME:** 30 MINUTES

Makes 4 servings

Sure, beef stroganoff is an old 20th-century favorite, the stuff of Grandma's and Mom's time along with Kelvinator refrigerators and Mixmaster hand mixers. Here, I resurrect this old favorite minus all unhealthy ingredients, creating a wonderful traditional dish for special occasions or a rich evening meal.

3 tablespoons butter, divided

1 pound sirloin or beef tenderloin, thinly sliced into ½" strips

12 ounces sliced mushrooms (button, cremini, or portobello)

3 shallots or 1 large yellow onion, sliced

2 cloves garlic, minced

½ cup beef broth

¼ teaspoon sea salt

¼ teaspoon ground black pepper

1 cup sour cream

1 tablespoon Dijon mustard

In a large skillet over medium-high heat, melt 1 tablespoon of the butter. Sear the beef for 2 minutes, turning once, or until browned on both sides and just barely cooked through. (Work in batches, if necessary.) Remove beef to a plate and set aside. Return the skillet to medium heat.

Add the remaining 2 tablespoons butter, the mushrooms, shallots or onion, and garlic. Cook for 5 minutes, or until the shallots or onion is softened and the mushrooms release their juices. Stir in the reserved beef, the broth, salt, and pepper. Bring to a boil, reduce the heat to medium-low, cover, and simmer for 10 minutes.

Stir in the sour cream and mustard. Cook for 1 minute, or until heated through.

PER SERVING: 353 calories, 29 g protein, 6 g carbohydrates, 24 g total fat, 13 g saturated fat, 1 g fiber, 406 mg sodium

VEAL SCHNITZEL WITH LEMON WINE SAUCE

PREP TIME: 10 MINUTES | **TOTAL TIME:** 30 MINUTES

Makes 4 servings

Rediscover this traditional Austrian dish in our wheat-free world using almond flour and ground golden flaxseeds as the "breading." Optionally, serve with mashed cauliflower.

Some grocery stores sell very thin veal cutlets. If you find thicker ones, pound them between 2 sheets of plastic wrap with a meat mallet or skillet to an even ¼" thickness.

2 **eggs**	1 **pound veal cutlets, ⅛"–¼" thick**
¾ **teaspoon sea salt, divided**	2 **tablespoons extra-virgin olive oil**
¾ **teaspoon ground black pepper, divided**	¼ **cup dry white wine or chicken broth**
½ **cup blanched almond flour**	2 **teaspoons lemon juice**
½ **cup ground golden flaxseeds**	1 **tablespoon fresh parsley, minced**
½ **teaspoon garlic powder**	2 **tablespoons butter, cubed and at room temperature**

Preheat the oven to 200°F.

In a shallow bowl or pie plate, lightly beat the eggs with ¼ teaspoon of the salt and ¼ teaspoon of the pepper.

In a separate shallow bowl or pie plate, combine the flour, flaxseeds, garlic powder, the remaining ½ teaspoon salt, and the remaining ½ teaspoon pepper. Dip the veal cutlets into the egg, shaking off any excess. Dredge in the flour mixture. Place the breaded cutlet on a plate. Repeat with the remaining cutlets.

In a large skillet over medium heat, heat the oil until hot. Cook the cutlets for 4 minutes, turning once, or until golden brown (add additional oil if necessary). Place the cooked cutlets on a baking sheet and keep warm in the oven.

Add the wine or broth and lemon juice to the skillet, using a wooden spoon to loosen any browned bits on the bottom. Cook, stirring, for 2 minutes. Stir in the parsley. Remove the skillet from the heat and whisk in the butter, 1 to 2 cubes at a time, until fully incorporated. Spoon the sauce over the cutlets.

PER SERVING: 387 calories, 32 g protein, 7 g carbohydrates, 26 g total fat, 4 g saturated fat, 6 g fiber, 441 mg sodium

BARBECUE BEEF QUESADILLAS

PREP TIME: 10 MINUTES | **TOTAL TIME:** 30 MINUTES

Makes 4 servings

The use of the Barbecue Sauce converts this dish, which is usually filled with sugar or high-fructose corn syrup, into something healthy but every bit as delicious as the original version. Serve as is, or with sour cream and guacamole.

- 2 tablespoons extra-virgin olive oil, divided
- 4 ounces strip, skirt, or rib-eye steak
- ½ teaspoon sea salt, divided
- ½ teaspoon ground black pepper, divided
- 1 yellow onion, quartered and thinly sliced
- 2 cloves garlic, minced
- 1 green bell pepper, seeded and thinly sliced
- ⅓ cup Barbecue Sauce (page 35)
- 8 Tortillas (page 29)
- 1 cup shredded Cheddar cheese

In a large skillet over medium heat, heat 1 tablespoon of the oil until hot. Season the steak with ¼ teaspoon of the salt and ¼ teaspoon of the black pepper. Sear the steak for 5 minutes, turning once, or until browned on both sides. Remove from the skillet and let rest for 5 minutes. Slice thinly.

Meanwhile, heat the remaining 1 tablespoon oil in the skillet. Cook the onion, garlic, bell pepper, the remaining ¼ teaspoon salt, and the remaining ¼ teaspoon black pepper for 5 minutes, stirring occasionally, or until the onion is translucent and the bell pepper softens. Remove from the heat, add the beef, and stir the barbecue sauce into the mixture.

Wipe the skillet clean and heat over medium heat. Place 1 tortilla in the center. Sprinkle 1 tablespoon cheese on the tortilla and top with one-fourth of the steak mixture. Sprinkle another tablespoon cheese over the steak mixture, and set another tortilla on top. Cook for 2 minutes, turning once, or until both tortillas are golden and the cheese is melted. Remove and cover to keep warm. Repeat with the remaining tortillas and filling.

PER SERVING: 579 calories, 32 g protein, 25 g carbohydrates, 43 g total fat, 10 g saturated fat, 14 g fiber, 845 mg sodium

KID-FRIENDLY

BEEF STEW

PREP TIME: 5 MINUTES | **TOTAL TIME:** 30 MINUTES

Makes 4 servings

Another old favorite from 20th-century Americana makes a comeback sans wheat. This updated version adds some hearty vegetables along with a red wine sauce for added richness and health benefits.

1 pound chuck roast, cut into 1" cubes

2 tablespoons chickpea flour or coconut flour

2 tablespoons extra-virgin olive oil

1 quart beef stock

1 bag (16 ounces) frozen vegetables (broccoli, cauliflower, and carrots)

2 teaspoons Italian Seasoning Mix (page 56)

1 teaspoon ground black pepper

½ teaspoon sea salt

¼ cup dry red wine

3 tablespoons tomato paste

In a large resealable plastic bag, combine the cubed beef and flour. Shake well until the beef is coated.

In a large saucepan, heat the oil over medium-high heat. Cook the beef, turning, for 10 minutes, or until browned on all sides.

Add the stock, vegetables, seasoning mix, pepper, salt, and wine and bring to a boil. Reduce the heat to a simmer and cook for 10 minutes.

Add the tomato paste and cook for 5 minutes, or until thickened.

PER SERVING: 317 calories, 30 g protein, 14 g carbohydrates, 13 g total fat, 3 g saturated fat, 4 g fiber, 502 mg sodium

UNSTUFFED CABBAGE AND BEEF

PREP TIME: 5 MINUTES | **TOTAL TIME:** 30 MINUTES

Makes 4 servings

Don't let the simplicity of this healthy, wheat-free recipe fool you: It yields a delicious and filling final product that you will be proud to serve! If desired, this can be served over "riced" cauliflower.

1 tablespoon olive oil	½ teaspoon sea salt
1 pound ground sirloin or ground round	½ teaspoon ground black pepper
1 small onion, chopped	1 bag (16 ounces) coleslaw mix
1 can (14.5 ounces) crushed tomatoes	½ cup water
	½ cup sour cream (optional)

In a large Dutch oven or skillet with a lid over medium-high heat, heat the oil. Cook the ground beef and onion, breaking the beef into small chunks, for 5 minutes, or until the beef is no longer pink and the onion is soft. Stir in the tomatoes, salt, and pepper. Add the coleslaw mix and water and stir until combined. Reduce the heat to medium, cover, and simmer, stirring occasionally, for 20 minutes, or until the cabbage is desired doneness.

Remove from the heat and stir in the sour cream, if desired. Taste for seasoning and add more salt and pepper, if needed.

PER SERVING: 227 calories, 26 g protein, 8 g carbohydrates, 10 g total fat, 2 g saturated fat, 3 g fiber, 374 mg sodium

SLOPPY JOES

PREP TIME: 10 MINUTES | **TOTAL TIME:** 30 MINUTES

Makes 4 servings

This perennial kid favorite is simple to make and easily fits into a wheat-free lifestyle. Make the wheat-free bread (for example, Basic Sandwich Muffins, page 24) ahead of time to top with this Sloppy Joe mix as an open-faced sandwich.

If you make the rolls at the same time as the Sloppy Joe mix, allow an additional 10 minutes to make the rolls from the All-Purpose Baking Mix (page 19) so they can bake while the Sloppy Joe mixture is cooking on the stove.

1 pound ground beef	1 can (8 ounces) tomato sauce
1 small onion, chopped	½ cup Barbecue Sauce (page 35)
1 green bell pepper, chopped	½ teaspoon sea salt
2 cloves garlic, minced, or 1 teaspoon garlic powder	

In a large skillet over medium-high heat, cook the beef for 5 minutes, or until no longer pink. Add the onion, pepper, and garlic or garlic powder and cook for 5 minutes, or until the vegetables soften. Drain. Reduce the heat to medium-low and stir in the tomato sauce, barbecue sauce, and salt. Cover and cook for 10 minutes.

PER SERVING: 301 calories, 23 g protein, 13 g carbohydrates, 18 g total fat, 7 g saturated fat, 2 g fiber, 728 mg sodium

TACO LETTUCE WRAPS

PREP TIME: 5 MINUTES | **TOTAL TIME:** 15 MINUTES

Makes 4 servings

Make light but tasty Mexican wraps, spiced up with time-saving Taco Seasoning Mix, using a wheat-free lettuce wrap. Optionally, add some sliced onions and green bell peppers to the ground beef.

Top the wrap filling with chopped avocado, shredded Cheddar cheese, chopped tomatoes, sour cream, or salsa.

1¼ pounds ground beef	8 large leaves lettuce (such as Bibb)
1 teaspoon Taco Seasoning Mix (page 57)	Toppings: chopped avocado, shredded Cheddar cheese, chopped tomatoes, sour cream, salsa
1 cup salsa	

In a large skillet over medium-high heat, cook the beef and seasoning mix, breaking the beef up with a large spoon, for 5 minutes, or until no longer pink. Reduce the heat to medium, stir in the salsa and cook for 3 minutes, or until most of the liquid has evaporated.

To serve, divide the meat filling evenly among the lettuce. Top with desired toppings. Roll up.

PER SERVING: 385 calories, 31 g protein, 15 g carbohydrates, 22 g total fat, 8 g saturated fat, 4 g fiber, 450 mg sodium

POBLANO PEPPER AND BEEF TORTILLAS

PREP TIME: 10 MINUTES | **TOTAL TIME:** 20 MINUTES

Makes 4 servings

Now that you can make tortillas without wheat or corn, well, let's put them to good use! Here is one simple way to combine the Mexican flavors of the Taco Seasoning Mix with the fresh flavor of a poblano chile pepper, topped with cheese, of course!

Serve these tortillas with your favorite taco toppings, if desired: shredded lettuce, sour cream, chopped avocados, or chopped fresh tomatoes.

2 tablespoons extra-virgin olive oil

1 onion, finely chopped

1 poblano chile pepper, finely chopped (wear plastic gloves when handling)

2 cloves garlic, minced

¾ pound ground beef

1 tablespoon Taco Seasoning Mix (page 57)

½ teaspoon sea salt

1 large tomato, chopped

4 Tortillas (page 29)

1 cup shredded taco or Cheddar cheese

In a large skillet over medium-high heat, heat the oil. Cook the onion, pepper, and garlic for 3 minutes, or until softened. Add the beef, seasoning mix, and salt and cook, stirring frequently, for 3 minutes, or until no longer pink.

Stir in the tomato, cover, and cook for 2 minutes, or until heated through. Spoon ½ cup of the beef mixture over each tortilla. Sprinkle each with ¼ cup cheese and fold.

PER SERVING: 641 calories, 41 g protein, 17 g carbohydrates, 47 g total fat, 17 g saturated fat, 8 g fiber, 881 mg sodium

MIDDLE EASTERN LAMB BURGERS

PREP TIME: 10 MINUTES | TOTAL TIME: 20 MINUTES

Makes 4 servings

These unique burgers are rich with an exotic mix of flavors from mint and the Moroccan blend of seasonings. They combine especially well with the Dilled Cucumber Yogurt Sauce (page 38).

1 pound ground lamb

1 large clove garlic, minced

1 small onion, grated

1 teaspoon dried mint

¾ teaspoon sea salt

1½ teaspoons Moroccan Seasoning Mix (page 48)

1 egg

2 tablespoons extra-virgin olive oil

In a medium bowl, combine the lamb, garlic, onion, mint, salt, seasoning mix, and egg until well combined. Divide the meat mixture into 4 burgers.

In a large skillet over medium heat, heat the oil until hot. Cook the patties for 8 minutes, turning once, or until browned and a thermometer inserted in the center registers 160°F for medium.

PER SERVING: 340 calories, 21 g protein, 5 g carbohydrates, 26 g total fat, 12 g saturated fat, 1 g fiber, 394 mg sodium

GRILLED PORK TENDERLOIN

PREP TIME: 5 MINUTES | **TOTAL TIME:** 20 MINUTES

Makes 4 servings

Enhanced with a seasoning mix (here I use the Cajun, but you can replace it with the Italian, Moroccan, Taco, or your own mix of herbs and spices), a delicious grilled pork tenderloin requires just a few minutes of preparation and 15 or so minutes of grilling.

1 tablespoon Cajun Seasoning Mix (page 58)

1 teaspoon sea salt

1½ pounds pork tenderloin

1 cup Barbecue Sauce (page 35), divided

Grease the grill rack or broiler-pan rack. If using a gas grill, set the heat at medium-high. If using a broiler, set the rack 6 to 8" from the heat source and preheat to high.

In a small bowl, combine the seasoning mix and salt.

Slice the silver skin off the pork (but leave the fat, it's good for you!). Rub the seasoning mixture into the pork. Place ½ cup of the barbecue sauce in a small bowl and set aside.

Place the pork on the grill or broiler pan. Grill or broil for 8 minutes, turning once. Brush with the remaining ½ cup barbecue sauce. Grill or broil for 7 minutes, turning once, or until a thermometer inserted in the center reaches 160°F and the juices run clear. Slice and serve with the reserved barbecue sauce.

PER SERVING: 222 calories, 36 g protein, 8 g carbohydrates, 4 g total fat, 1 g saturated fat, 1 g fiber, 753 mg sodium

DIJON MUSTARD PORK TENDERLOIN MEDALLIONS

PREP TIME: 5 MINUTES | **TOTAL TIME:** 25 MINUTES

Makes 4 servings

Pork tenderloin is a pretty classy dish to start with. But here's an even classier combination of Dijon mustard and white wine that your family and guests will think required hours to prepare. For greatest flavor, leave the fat on the tenderloin.

2 tablespoons extra-virgin olive oil

1½ pounds pork tenderloin, cut into ½- to ¾"-thick slices

1 shallot, minced

8 ounces portobello mushrooms, thinly sliced

¼ cup Dijon mustard

¼ cup heavy cream or canned coconut milk

2 tablespoons white wine

½ teaspoon sea salt

In a large skillet over high heat, heat the oil. Working in batches if necessary, cook the pork slices for 4 minutes, turning once, or until browned. Transfer to a plate.

Reduce the heat to medium. Cook the shallot and mushrooms, stirring frequently, for 5 minutes, or until the mushrooms are softened. Stir in the mustard, cream or coconut milk, wine, and salt. Cook for 4 minutes, stirring occasionally, or until blended. Return the pork medallions to the skillet, cover, and cook for 5 minutes, or until the flavors blend and the pork is cooked through.

PER SERVING: 353 calories, 38 g protein, 10 g carbohydrates, 16 g total fat, 6 g saturated fat, 1 g fiber, 657 mg sodium

ITALIAN ROASTED PORK TENDERLOIN

PREP TIME: 5 MINUTES | **TOTAL TIME:** 30 MINUTES

Makes 4 servings

Pork tenderloin is an easy, delicious cut of meat that eagerly takes on the flavors of herbs and spices that surround it. The combined herbs of the Italian Seasoning Mix are used in this dish. For best flavor, don't trim the fat off the tenderloin.

This dish makes great leftovers for lunch, or even breakfast.

2 tablespoons extra-virgin olive oil

1½ pounds pork tenderloin

4 cloves garlic, minced

1 can (14 ounces) quartered artichoke hearts, drained

1 cup roasted red bell peppers, sliced

1 onion, halved and sliced

2 teaspoons Italian Seasoning Mix (page 56)

In a large skillet over medium-high heat, heat the oil. Cook the pork, turning as necessary, for 15 minutes, or until a thermometer inserted in the center reaches 160°F and the juices run clear. Transfer to a serving plate and cover with foil to keep warm.

Reduce the heat to medium. Cook the garlic, artichokes, peppers, onion, and seasoning mix, stirring occasionally, for 10 minutes, or until the onion is softened. Serve the vegetables with the pork.

PER SERVING: 310 calories, 38 g protein, 14 g carbohydrates, 11 g total fat, 2 g saturated fat, 3 g fiber, 494 mg sodium

SRIRACHA PORK AND EGGPLANT

PREP TIME: 15 MINUTES | **TOTAL TIME:** 30 MINUTES

Makes 4 servings

If you are a fan of hot pepper, you will love this extra-spicy pork and eggplant dish exploding with the unique flavors of Sriracha sauce. But be warned: This is for the true lover of hot and spicy! Or, reduce the Sriracha to 1 tablespoon to still get the delicious flavors without all the fire.

3 tablespoons extra-virgin olive oil or coconut oil, divided

1½ pounds pork tenderloin, cut into 1" cubes

1 eggplant, cut into ½" cubes

1 large yellow onion, halved and thinly sliced

1 large green bell pepper, thinly sliced

2–4 tablespoons Sriracha sauce

½ cup water

In a large skillet over medium-high heat, heat 1 tablespoon of the oil. Cook the pork for 5 minutes, turning occasionally, or until browned. Remove to a plate. Add the remaining 2 tablespoons oil to the skillet. Cook the eggplant, onion, and pepper for 3 minutes, stirring constantly. Stir in the Sriracha sauce, water, pork, and any accumulated juices. Reduce the heat to medium, cover, and cook for 10 minutes, stirring occasionally, or until the vegetables are softened and the pork is cooked through.

PER SERVING: 345 calories, 38 g protein, 15 g carbohydrates, 15 g total fat, 3 g saturated fat, 5 g fiber, 247 mg sodium

PORK MEDALLIONS WITH CIDER PAN SAUCE

PREP TIME: 15 MINUTES | **TOTAL TIME:** 25 MINUTES

Makes 4 servings

This pork dish is substantial enough to serve at holidays or to make an extra-special evening meal. The reduced apple juice and apple cider vinegar, along with thyme and butter, provide a rich dimension to the meaty flavors of the pork tenderloin. Don't trim the fat off your tenderloin, by the way, for added flavor.

Optionally, serve this dish with Buttered Cabbage (page 123).

½ cup almond meal/flour	2 tablespoons extra-virgin olive oil
¼ teaspoon sea salt	2 tablespoons butter, divided
¼ teaspoon dried thyme	1 shallot, minced
1½ pounds pork tenderloin, cut into ¼" slices	1 cup apple juice (no sugar added)
	2 tablespoons apple cider vinegar

On a plate, combine the flour, salt, and thyme. Dredge each pork medallion in the flour mixture to coat lightly and shake off excess.

In a large skillet over medium-high heat, heat the oil. Cook the pork for 3 minutes, turning once, or until golden brown. Transfer to a plate and loosely cover with foil to keep warm.

In the same skillet, melt 1 tablespoon of the butter. Cook the shallot, stirring constantly, for 1 minute, or until it begins to soften. Add the apple juice and vinegar and cook for 2 minutes, stirring to loosen any brown bits on the bottom of the skillet. Reduce the heat to medium-low and simmer for 5 minutes, or until the sauce has reduced by half. Stir in the remaining 1 tablespoon butter until melted.

Return the pork to the skillet, along with any accumulated juices, and heat for 1 minute, or until heated through.

PER SERVING: 421 calories, 39 g protein, 13 g carbohydrates, 24 g total fat, 6 g saturated fat, 2 g fiber, 247 mg sodium

JAMBALAYA

Makes 4 servings

Treat your family to this little hint of New Orleans spicy Cajun-style cooking while devoting just a few minutes to the effort!

While there are many variations on the traditional Creole dish, this version is free of wheat and sugars. It can be served as is alongside a steamed vegetable, or on top of "riced" cauliflower.

3 tablespoons extra-virgin olive oil or coconut oil, divided

1 yellow onion, finely chopped

2 cloves garlic, minced

1 jalapeño chile pepper, seeded and minced (wear plastic gloves when handling)

1 pound andouille sausage, sliced

8 ounces chicken breast, cut into 1" cubes

1–2 tablespoons Cajun Seasoning Mix (page 58)

1 can (14.5 ounces) diced tomatoes

1 package (6 ounces) fresh baby spinach

In a large skillet over medium-high heat, heat 2 tablespoons of the oil until hot. Cook the onion, garlic, and pepper for 3 minutes, or until they begin to soften.

Add the remaining 1 tablespoon oil to the skillet. Stir in the sausage and chicken. Cover and cook for 5 minutes, stirring occasionally, or until the chicken and sausage are almost cooked through. Stir in the seasoning mix, tomatoes with their juice, and spinach. Cover, reduce the heat to medium-low, and cook for 5 minutes, stirring once, or until the chicken and sausage are cooked through.

PER SERVING: 443 calories, 34 g protein, 14g carbohydrates, 28 g total fat, 8g saturated fat, 4 g fiber, 1,237 mg sodium

PEPPERS STUFFED WITH ITALIAN SAUSAGE

PREP TIME: 10 MINUTES | **TOTAL TIME:** 30 MINUTES

Makes 4 servings

While I love stuffed peppers, I don't like the time required to bake them nor the typical use of carbohydrate-rich stuffing contents. So here is a version of stuffed green peppers with some time-saving maneuvers built in, along with no grains used in the stuffing. This recipe makes enough ultrasaucy mixture to coat shirataki spaghetti or riced cauliflower.

2 tablespoons extra-virgin olive oil

1 pound ground Italian sausage

1 small yellow onion, finely chopped

2 cloves garlic, minced

1 teaspoon Italian Seasoning Mix (page 56)

1 can (14.5 ounces) diced tomatoes

1 jar (16 ounces) marinara sauce, divided

4 green bell peppers, tops and cores removed

1 tablespoon water

Preheat the oven to 375°F.

In a large skillet over medium heat, heat the oil. Cook the sausage, onion, garlic, and seasoning mix for 5 minutes, or until the sausage is browned and the onion is soft. Stir in the tomatoes with their juice and half the sauce, cover, and cook for 5 minutes.

Meanwhile, place the peppers in a microwaveable 9" glass pie plate or an 8" x 8" glass baking dish. Add the water, then microwave on high power for 5 minutes, or until the peppers are very soft.

Spoon the sausage mixture into the peppers. Pour the remaining tomato sauce over the peppers. Bake for 10 minutes, or until heated through.

PER SERVING: 318 calories, 22 g protein, 21 g carbohydrates, 17 g total fat, 5 g saturated fat, 5 g fiber, 1,475 mg sodium

PEPPER PIZZAS

PREP TIME: 5 MINUTES | **TOTAL TIME:** 25 MINUTES

Makes 4 servings

This is a variation on the stuffed pepper theme that tastes and smells like pizza! The mixture can be varied in many different ways. For instance, replace the Italian sausage with ground beef or turkey, or add Taco Seasoning Mix (page 57) and use a Mexican cheese blend in place of the mozzarella.

2 tablespoons extra-virgin olive oil

1 pound Italian sausage, loose or finely chopped

1½ cups pizza sauce

4 large yellow bell peppers, halved

4 tablespoons water, divided

1 cup shredded mozzarella cheese

Preheat the oven to 375°F.

In a large skillet over medium heat, heat the oil. Cook the sausage, stirring constantly, for 5 minutes, or until browned. Stir in the pizza sauce. Cover and cook for 5 minutes.

Meanwhile, place the peppers in 2 microwaveable 9" glass pie plates or 8" x 8" glass baking dishes. Add 1 tablespoon water to each, then microwave separately on high power for 5 minutes, or until the peppers are soft.

Spoon the sausage mixture equally into the peppers. Top with the cheese and bake for 5 minutes, or until the cheese melts.

PER SERVING: 393 calories, 30 g protein, 21 g carbohydrates, 23 g total fat, 8 g saturated fat, 5 g fiber, 1,290 mg sodium

PROVOLONE, PROSCIUTTO, AND KALAMATA OLIVE PIZZA

PREP TIME: 10 MINUTES | TOTAL TIME: 30 MINUTES

Makes 4 servings

The flavor combinations of this pizza may be better suited to adult palates. A kid-friendly version can be made by replacing prosciutto with sliced salami or sausage and replacing the provolone with additional mozzarella.

PIZZA CRUST

- 2½ cups All-Purpose Baking Mix (page 19)
- ½ cup shredded mozzarella cheese
- 1 egg
- 2 tablespoons extra-virgin olive oil
- ½ cup water

TOPPING

- 2 ounces provolone, cut into cubes
- ½ cup shredded mozzarella cheese
- ⅔ cup pizza sauce (no sugar added)
- 2 ounces prosciutto, cut into 1" pieces
- ½ cup pitted kalamata olives, halved
- 1 teaspoon red-pepper flakes (optional)

Preheat the oven to 400°F. Line a baking sheet or pizza pan with parchment paper.

To make the crust: In a medium bowl, combine the baking mix and cheese. In a small bowl, mix together the egg, oil, and water. Pour into the flour mixture and combine thoroughly.

Lay the dough on the baking sheet or pizza pan and, with moistened hands, press into a 12" circle, forming an outer edge. Bake for 10 minutes. Reduce the heat to 350°F.

To make the topping: In a small bowl, combine the provolone and mozzarella. Remove the pizza crust from the oven and top with the sauce, cheese mixture, prosciutto, olives, and pepper flakes, if desired. Bake for 10 minutes, or until the cheese melts.

PER SERVING: 703 calories, 31 g protein, 24 g carbohydrates, 58 g total fat, 11 g saturated fat, 12 g fiber, 1,288 mg sodium

MOROCCAN CHICKEN
WITH ROASTED BELL PEPPERS

PREP TIME: 10 MINUTES | **TOTAL TIME:** 30 MINUTES

Makes 4 servings

The exotic combination of seasonings in the Moroccan Seasoning Mix will have your family thinking you slaved over the stove for hours to achieve this unique mixture of flavors, when in reality it took 30 minutes!

1 tablespoon Moroccan Seasoning Mix (page 55)

1 teaspoon sea salt

4 boneless, skinless chicken breast halves

¼ cup extra-virgin olive oil, divided

1 yellow onion, quartered and sliced

8 ounces cremini (or baby bella) mushrooms, quartered

1 jar (7 ounces) roasted red bell peppers, drained and cut into ½"-thick slices

In a small bowl, combine the seasoning mix and salt. Rub half the mixture on the chicken breasts.

In a large skillet over medium-high heat, heat 2 tablespoons of the oil until hot. Cook the chicken for 5 minutes, turning, or until browned on both sides. Remove to a plate and set aside.

Add the remaining 2 tablespoons oil, the onion, mushrooms, and the remaining spice mixture to the skillet. Cook for 5 minutes, or until the vegetables are browned.

Add the reserved chicken back to the skillet along with the peppers. Reduce the heat to medium-low, cover, and simmer for 10 minutes, or until a thermometer inserted in the thickest portion of the chicken registers 165°F and the juices run clear.

PER SERVING: 354 calories, 38 g protein, 8 g carbohydrates, 19 g total fat, 3 g saturated fat, 2 g fiber, 620 mg sodium

SPICY CHICKEN THIGHS

PREP TIME: 5 MINUTES | **TOTAL TIME:** 30 MINUTES

Makes 8 servings

Since chicken wings take longer than 30 minutes to prepare, using boneless thighs allows for all the great flavor in less time. If you prefer a more mellow heat, this recipe also works if you dip the chicken thighs in the sauce mixture before baking. The sauce is also great on chicken wings. Change up this recipe by brushing the thighs with Barbecue Sauce (page 35) or Ginger-Miso Sauce (page 37) instead of the butter mixture.

Serve these spicy thighs as is or with Ranch Dressing (page 45) or sugar-free blue cheese dressing for dipping.

3 pounds boneless, skinless chicken thighs	**½** teaspoon ground black pepper
½ teaspoon sea salt	**¼** cup butter, melted
	¼ cup hot-pepper sauce

Preheat the oven to 425°F.

Place the chicken thighs on a rimmed baking sheet. Sprinkle with the salt and black pepper. Bake for 20 minutes, or until a thermometer inserted in the thickest portion registers 165°F and the juices run clear.

Meanwhile, in a large bowl, combine the melted butter and hot-pepper sauce. Add the hot chicken and toss to coat.

PER SERVING: 509 calories, 66 g protein, 0 g carbohydrates, 26 g total fat, 11 g saturated fat, 0 g fiber, 1,072 mg sodium

THAI RED CURRY CHICKEN

PREP TIME: 10 MINUTES | TOTAL TIME: 30 MINUTES

Makes 4 servings

Thai dishes make use of the wonderful properties of coconut, the unsung hero of the wheat-free world. This Thai Red Curry Chicken can be made as spicy hot as you like by adjusting the quantity of red curry paste you add to the Thai Red Curry Sauce.

For variety, other vegetables can be added or substituted, such as sliced zucchini, sliced carrots, or snap peas. Likewise, pork or beef can be substituted for chicken.

2 tablespoons coconut oil

1½ pounds boneless, skinless chicken breasts, cut into 1" strips

3 cloves garlic, minced

5 scallions, chopped

1 red bell pepper, thinly sliced

4 ounces sliced shiitake mushrooms

1 can (8 ounces) sliced bamboo shoots, drained

¾ cup Thai Red Curry Sauce (page 36)

¼ cup chopped cilantro or Thai basil

In a large skillet over medium-high heat, heat the oil. Cook the chicken for 5 minutes, or until beginning to brown on all sides, but not completely cooked through. Transfer to a plate and set aside.

Add the garlic, scallions, pepper, mushrooms, and bamboo shoots to the skillet. Cook, stirring constantly, for 3 minutes, or until the pepper is lightly browned. Add the reserved chicken, along with accumulated juices, and the curry sauce. Stir to partially submerge the chicken in the liquid. Reduce the heat to medium, cover, and cook, stirring occasionally, for 10 minutes, or until the chicken is cooked through. Stir in the cilantro or basil.

PER SERVING: 490 calories, 41 g protein, 12 g carbohydrates, 32 g total fat, 25 g saturated fat, 4 g fiber, 566 mg sodium

GINGER-MISO CHICKEN

PREP TIME: 5 MINUTES | **TOTAL TIME:** 20 MINUTES

Makes 4 servings

Preparation time is slashed on this Asian-style chicken rich with the flavors of ginger, miso, wasabi, and sesame by using the prepared Ginger-Miso Sauce. Serve alongside steamed spinach or atop shirataki noodles or "riced" cauliflower.

3 tablespoons extra-virgin olive oil or coconut oil, divided

1½ pounds chicken cutlets

4 scallions, sliced

8 ounces sliced shiitake mushrooms

½ cup Ginger-Miso Sauce (page 37)

In a large skillet over medium-high heat, heat 2 tablespoons of the oil. Cook the chicken for 2 minutes, turning once, or until browned. Work in batches, if necessary. Transfer to a plate and set aside.

Reduce the heat to medium. Add the remaining 1 tablespoon oil to the skillet. Cook the scallions and mushrooms, stirring, for 2 minutes, or until the mushrooms are lightly browned. Place the reserved chicken on top of the vegetables, and pour the ginger sauce over the chicken. Cover and cook for 10 minutes, or until the chicken is no longer pink and the juices run clear.

PER SERVING: 412 calories, 39 g protein, 8 g carbohydrates, 24 g total fat, 3 g saturated fat, 3 g fiber, 492 mg sodium

MAPLE-PECAN CHICKEN

PREP TIME: 10 MINUTES | **TOTAL TIME:** 20 MINUTES

Makes 4 servings

A sweet and crunchy coating makes this quick and easy chicken cutlet recipe a kid-friendly dish.

The pecan meal can be purchased preground, or you can simply grind whole nuts in your food processor, food chopper, or coffee grinder.

½ cup pecan meal or ground pecans

¼ teaspoon sea salt

2 tablespoons butter, melted

1 tablespoon sugar-free maple-flavored syrup

1 pound chicken cutlets

1 tablespoon butter

1 tablespoon olive oil

In a shallow bowl or pie plate, combine the pecan meal or ground pecans and the salt. In a separate shallow bowl or pie plate, combine the 2 tablespoons melted butter and the syrup. Dip each cutlet into the butter mixture, evenly coating both sides. Dredge in the pecan mixture, pressing lightly to coat both sides.

In a large skillet over medium heat, heat 1 tablespoon butter and the oil until hot. Cook the chicken for 8 minutes, turning once, or until the chicken is no longer pink, and the juices run clear.

PER SERVING: 290 calories, 25 g protein, 2 g carbohydrates, 20 g total fat, 7 g saturated fat, 1 g fiber, 353 mg sodium

KID-FRIENDLY

BARBECUE BACON-WRAPPED CHICKEN

PREP TIME: 10 MINUTES | **TOTAL TIME:** 25 MINUTES

Makes 4 servings

Quick and easy, this nutritionally complete meal has something to satisfy every family member. The bacon makes the chicken perfectly compatible with breakfast if there are leftovers!

4 boneless, skinless chicken breast halves

12 slices bacon

4 ounces cherry tomatoes, halved (¾ cup)

8 scallions, cut into 2" pieces

⅛ teaspoon sea salt

½ cup Barbecue Sauce (page 35)

Place the oven rack 6" from the heat source and preheat the broiler. Line a baking sheet or broiler pan with foil.

Wrap 3 slices of bacon around each chicken breast half and set on the baking sheet or broiler pan.

Broil for 6 minutes, or until the bacon begins to crisp and brown. Remove from the oven and turn the chicken over. Scatter the tomatoes and scallions around the chicken and sprinkle with the salt. Return to the oven and broil for 6 minutes, or until the bacon is cooked through and a thermometer inserted in the thickest portion of the chicken registers 165°F and the juices run clear.

Spoon 2 tablespoons of the barbecue sauce over each chicken breast half. Stir the vegetables and broil for 1 minute.

PER SERVING: 545 calories, 45 g protein, 11 g carbohydrates, 37 g total fat, 13 g saturated fat, 2 g fiber, 875 mg sodium

CAJUN CHICKEN CUTLETS

PREP TIME: 5 MINUTES | TOTAL TIME: 20 MINUTES

Makes 4 servings

I economize on time with this spicy-hot Cajun chicken dish by using the Cajun Seasoning Mix.

This dish goes exceptionally well over Spinach Gratin.

3 tablespoons Mayonnaise (page 40 or store-bought)

2 tablespoons almond meal/flour

1 tablespoon Cajun Seasoning Mix (page 58)

1 teaspoon Sriracha or hot-pepper sauce (optional)

½ teaspoon sea salt

4 boneless, skinless chicken breast halves

Spinach Gratin (optional, page 128)

Preheat the oven to 425°F. Line a baking sheet with parchment paper or foil.

In a small bowl, combine the mayonnaise, almond meal/flour, seasoning mix, Sriracha or hot-pepper sauce (if desired), and salt.

Place the chicken breasts on the baking sheet and brush the tops evenly with the mayonnaise mixture.

Bake for 15 minutes, or until a thermometer inserted in the thickest portion registers 165°F and the juices run clear. If additional browning is desired, broil for 2 to 3 minutes. If serving with Spinach Gratin, prepare the spinach while the chicken is baking.

PER SERVING: 263 calories, 31 g protein, 2 g carbohydrates, 14 g total fat, 2 g saturated fat, 1 g fiber, 517 mg sodium

CHICKEN PICCATA

PREP TIME: 5 MINUTES | **TOTAL TIME:** 30 MINUTES

Makes 4 servings

The classic *piccata* method of slicing, coating, and sautéing meat in a piquant sauce makes a comeback in a wheat-free, healthy version. Olive oil, lemon, capers, and butter create that familiar rich Italian flavor that goes so well with steamed green vegetables, mushrooms sautéed in butter, or "riced" cauliflower.

The chicken can be replaced by veal, pork chops, white fish, or sliced eggplant.

½ cup almond meal/flour

¼ teaspoon sea salt

1¼ pounds chicken cutlets

¼ cup extra-virgin olive oil

½ cup chicken broth

1 medium shallot, minced, or 1 large clove garlic, minced

¼ cup lemon juice

2 tablespoons capers

3 tablespoons unsalted butter, sliced

2 tablespoons chopped fresh parsley

In a shallow bowl or pie plate, combine the almond meal/flour and salt. Dredge the chicken cutlets in the flour mixture, shaking off any excess.

In a large skillet over medium heat, heat the oil until hot. Working in batches if necessary, cook the chicken, for 6 minutes, turning once, or until golden brown and the chicken is no longer pink and the juices run clear. Transfer to a warm platter and cover loosely with foil.

Add the broth and shallot or garlic to the skillet, increase the heat to high, and cook, stirring with a wooden spoon or spatula to loosen any browned bits. Boil for 4 minutes, or until the broth has reduced by half. Add the lemon juice and capers and continue simmering for 2 minutes. Remove from the heat and add the butter, stirring until the butter melts and thickens the sauce. Stir in the parsley. Spoon the sauce over the chicken.

PER SERVING: 462 calories, 35 g protein, 4 g carbohydrates, 34 g total fat, 9 g saturated fat, 2 g fiber, 485 mg sodium

CHICKEN PAPRIKASH

PREP TIME: 10 MINUTES | TOTAL TIME: 30 MINUTES

Makes 4 servings

The flavor of this traditional Hungarian dish is defined by the red bell pepper and paprika, which highlight the flavor background of chicken, onion, and sour cream. Therefore, use the freshest and sweetest red bell pepper and the best-quality paprika that fits in your budget.

This dish goes well over Zucchini Noodles (page 130).

2 tablespoons extra-virgin olive oil	2 tablespoons smoked paprika
1 onion, thinly sliced	½ teaspoon sea salt
1 large red bell pepper, thinly sliced	½ cup chicken broth
1½ pounds chicken tenders	1 cup sour cream
2 cloves garlic, minced	

In a large skillet over medium-high heat, heat the oil until hot. Cook the onion and pepper, stirring frequently, for 5 minutes, or until lightly browned. Add the chicken and cook for 5 minutes, turning, or until browned. Add the garlic, paprika, and salt and cook, stirring constantly, for 2 minutes.

Add the broth. Bring to a simmer. Reduce the heat to medium-low, cover, and simmer for 5 minutes, or until the chicken is no longer pink and the juices run clear. Stir in the sour cream.

PER SERVING: 396 calories, 39 g protein, 10 g carbohydrates, 22 g total fat, 8 g saturated fat, 3 g fiber, 481 mg sodium

ROASTED RED PEPPER CHICKEN ALFREDO

PREP TIME: 10 MINUTES | **TOTAL TIME:** 25 MINUTES

4 servings

Here is a wheat-free, dairy-free version of chicken in a creamy Alfredo sauce that also folds in the delightful flavor of roasted red pepper.

1 can (14 ounces) coconut milk

1 large roasted red pepper (from a jar), roughly chopped

3 packages (8 ounces each) shirataki fettuccine, rinsed and drained

2 tablespoons extra-virgin olive oil

1 pound chicken tenders, cut into 1" pieces

½ teaspoon sea salt

3 cloves garlic, minced

½ cup grated Parmesan cheese

2 tablespoons chopped fresh basil

In a blender or food processor, combine the coconut milk and pepper. Blend or process for 1 minute and set aside.

Prepare the fettuccine according to package directions. Drain.

Meanwhile, in a large saucepan over medium-high heat, heat the oil until hot. Sprinkle the chicken with the salt and cook for 5 minutes, or until the chicken is barely pink. Add the garlic and cook, stirring, for 1 minute. Add the reserved coconut milk mixture.

Heat just until the mixture begins to boil, reduce the heat to medium-low, and simmer for 5 minutes. Stir in the cheese and basil and cook for 2 minutes or until the sauce thickens slightly. Add the fettuccine and toss to coat well.

PER SERVING: 441 calories, 30 g protein, 6 g carbohydrates, 34 g total fat, 22 g saturated fat, 2 g fiber, 503 mg sodium

CAJUN TURKEY BURGERS

PREP TIME: 5 MINUTES | **TOTAL TIME:** 15 MINUTES

Makes 4 burgers

These turkey burgers explode with the spicy flavors of the Cajun Seasoning Mix. If the seasoning is premade, these burgers can be on the table in 15 minutes. For a change of pace, substitute any of the other seasoning mixes.

Serve topped with Monterey Jack, Asiago, or Cheddar cheese, sliced tomato, and arugula, either with or without being sandwiched inside Basic Sandwich Muffins (page 27).

1 pound ground turkey

2 tablespoons Cajun Seasoning Mix (page 58)

1 tablespoon hot-pepper sauce (optional)

2 tablespoons extra-virgin olive oil or coconut oil

In a large bowl, combine the turkey, seasoning mix, and hot-pepper sauce (if desired) and mix thoroughly. Form into 4 burgers.

In a large skillet over medium heat, heat the oil until hot. Cook the burgers for 8 minutes, turning once, or until a thermometer inserted in the center registers 165°F and the meat is no longer pink.

PER SERVING: 239 calories, 23 g protein, 2 g carbohydrates, 16 g total fat, 3 g saturated fat, 1 g fiber, 271 mg sodium

MISO-GLAZED ORANGE ROUGHY

PREP TIME: 5 MINUTES | **TOTAL TIME:** 20 MINUTES

Makes 4 servings

The tangy Asian flavors of the Ginger-Miso Sauce are put to use to create this fish dish in a snap.

Any white fish can be substituted for the orange roughy, such as cod, haddock, flounder, or trout.

1½ **pounds orange roughy fillets**

¼ **cup Ginger-Miso Sauce (page 37)**

1 **tablespoon chopped cilantro, for garnish**

Preheat the oven to 375°F.

Arrange the fish fillets in a 13" x 9" baking dish. Cover each with the ginger sauce. Bake for 15 minutes, or until the fish flakes easily. Serve sprinkled with the cilantro, if desired.

PER SERVING: 136 calories, 20 g protein, 1 g carbohydrates, 5 g total fat, 0.5 g saturated fat, 0 g fiber, 226 mg sodium

CAJUN BAKED FISH WITH SHRIMP CREAM SAUCE

PREP TIME: 5 MINUTES | TOTAL TIME: 20 MINUTES

Makes 4 servings

The peppery Cajun Seasoning Mix and creamy sauce with shrimp liven up the light flavors of any white fish, such as cod, haddock, flounder, or orange roughy.

FISH

- 4 cod, haddock, or other firm white fish fillets (1 pound)
- 2 tablespoons butter, melted
- 2 teaspoons lemon juice
- 1 teaspoon Cajun Seasoning Mix (page 58)

SAUCE

- 2 tablespoons butter, divided
- ¼ pound peeled and deveined medium shrimp, chopped
- 2 tablespoons snipped chives
- 3 ounces cream cheese, cubed
- 1 cup cream or half-and-half
- ⅛ teaspoon sea salt

To make the fish: Preheat the oven to 375°F. Grease a 13" x 9" baking dish.

Place the fish fillets in the baking dish. In a small bowl, combine the melted butter, lemon juice, and seasoning mix. Brush the butter mixture on the fillets. Bake for 15 minutes, or until the fish flakes easily. While the fish is baking, prepare the shrimp cream sauce.

To make the sauce: In a medium skillet over medium-high heat, melt 1 tablespoon of the butter. Cook the shrimp and chives, stirring frequently, for 2 minutes, or just until the shrimp turn pink. Push the shrimp toward the outer edges of the skillet and reduce the heat to medium-low. Add the remaining 1 tablespoon butter and the cream cheese to the center of the skillet, stirring until softened and melted. Add the cream or half-and-half and salt. Simmer, stirring frequently, for 5 minutes, or until the sauce bubbles gently and thickens. Remove from the heat.

Serve the fillets topped with the shrimp cream sauce.

PER SERVING: 407 calories, 27 g protein, 4 g carbohydrates, 31 g total fat, 19 g saturated fat, 0 g fiber, 483 mg sodium

PARMESAN-CRUSTED COD

PREP TIME: 5 MINUTES | **TOTAL TIME:** 20 MINUTES

Makes 4 servings

The combination of grated Parmesan cheese and Italian Seasoning Mix can put any conventional breading to shame! Tilapia can be substituted for the cod, if desired.

¼ cup grated Parmesan cheese

½ teaspoon Italian Seasoning Mix (page 56)

1½ pounds cod, cut into 4 pieces

2 tablespoons olive oil

Preheat the oven to 375°F.

In a small bowl, combine the cheese and seasoning mix.

Arrange the cod in a 13" x 9" baking dish. Brush with the oil and top with the cheese mixture.

Bake for 15 minutes, or until the fish flakes easily.

PER SERVING: 175 calories, 22 g protein, 1 g carbohydrates, 9 g total fat, 2 g saturated fat, 0 g fiber, 138 mg sodium

KID-FRIENDLY

FILLET OF FISH AMANDINE

PREP TIME: 10 MINUTES | **TOTAL TIME:** 20 MINUTES

Makes 4 servings

Here's a re-creation of a classic white fish recipe, the sort that just crumbles apart with your fork and bursts open with the heady combined scents and flavors of lemon, butter, and fish, with crunch provided by toasted almonds.

Fillet of sole, flounder, or other white fish can be substituted for the tilapia.

½ cup almond meal/flour

¼ teaspoon onion powder

¼ teaspoon sea salt

⅛ teaspoon ground red pepper (optional)

4 tilapia fillets (1 pound)

3 tablespoons extra-virgin olive oil, divided

½ cup sliced almonds

1 tablespoon butter

2 tablespoons lemon juice

4 lemon wedges

Preheat the oven to 350°F.

In a shallow bowl or pie plate, combine the almond meal/flour, onion powder, salt, and red pepper (if desired). Dredge the fish in the mixture, pressing lightly to evenly coat both sides.

In a large skillet over medium-high heat, heat 2 tablespoons of the oil until hot. Cook the fillets (with the thicker parts toward the center of the skillet) for 10 minutes, turning once. Add the remaining 1 tablespoon oil to the skillet and cook until the fish flakes easily.

Meanwhile, spread the almonds in a shallow baking dish and bake for 5 minutes, or until golden.

Carefully remove the cooked fillets to a platter. Add the butter to the hot skillet and stir in the toasted almonds, tossing to coat with the butter. Add the lemon juice and stir. Spoon the buttered almonds and any remaining pan juices over each fillet. Serve with lemon wedges.

PER SERVING: 354 calories, 26 g protein, 6 g carbohydrates, 26 g total fat, 6 g saturated fat, 3 g fiber, 215 mg sodium

COCONUT-CRUSTED FISH STICKS

PREP TIME: 10 MINUTES | **TOTAL TIME:** 25 MINUTES

Makes 4 servings

These crunchy coconut-crusted fish sticks are a kid-friendly way to get the family to eat more healthy fish. For a cheesy coating, add a tablespoon of grated Parmesan cheese to the coconut.

Serve with coleslaw or steamed vegetables.

¾ cup unsweetened shredded coconut

⅓ cup ground golden flaxseeds

½ teaspoon sea salt

¼ cup butter, melted

1 pound cod or haddock fillets, cut into ½" x 3" sticks

Preheat the oven to 400°F. Set a baking rack inside a baking sheet and coat with olive oil or coconut oil.

In a shallow bowl or pie plate, combine the coconut, flaxseeds, and salt. Place the melted butter in a shallow bowl. Dip the fish sticks in the melted butter, shaking off the excess. Dredge in the coconut mixture, turning to coat. Place on the baking rack. Coat lightly with cooking spray or brush with olive or coconut oil.

Bake for 15 minutes, or until the coating is golden and the fish flakes easily.

PER SERVING: 365 calories, 23 g protein, 7 g carbohydrates, 27 g total fat, 17 g saturated fat, 5 g fiber, 460 mg sodium

SEARED SALMON OVER SESAME SPINACH

PREP TIME: 5 MINUTES | **TOTAL TIME:** 15 MINUTES

Makes 4 servings

Time is saved with this quick but elegant seared salmon recipe by using just one skillet. If you're not in a rush, you can steam the spinach separately, drain it, and then add the Ginger-Miso Sauce.

1 tablespoon coconut oil

4 salmon steaks (about 8 ounces each)

2 packages (6 ounces each) fresh spinach

½ cup Ginger-Miso Sauce (page 37)

In a large skillet over medium-high heat, heat the oil. Cook the salmon steaks for 5 minutes. Turn and top with the spinach. Pour the sesame sauce over the spinach. Cover and cook for 3 minutes, or until the salmon is opaque and the spinach is wilted.

Serve the spinach with the salmon placed on top, drizzled with any pan juices.

PER SERVING: 570 calories, 46 g protein, 5 g carbohydrates, 40 g total fat, 10 g saturated fat, 2 g fiber, 464 mg sodium

SALMON CROQUETTES

PREP TIME: 10 MINUTES | **TOTAL TIME:** 20 MINUTES

Makes 4 servings

The lively flavors of the Herbes de Provence bring simple canned salmon to life in this re-imagined version of fish cakes.

¼ cup Mayonnaise (page 40 or store-bought)

1 rib celery, finely diced

1 tablespoon fresh lemon juice

1 teaspoon Herbes de Provence (page 59)

¾ teaspoon mustard powder

2 cans (6 ounces each) skinless and boneless pink salmon, drained and flaked

1 egg, lightly beaten

½ cup ground golden flaxseeds

2 tablespoons extra-virgin olive oil

8 teaspoons Garlicky Mayo Spread (page 41)

In a medium bowl, combine the mayonnaise, celery, lemon juice, Herbes de Provence, mustard, salmon, egg, and flaxseeds. Mix well. Shape into eight 2" patties.

In a large skillet over medium heat, heat the oil. Cook the patties for 6 minutes, turning once, or until golden brown. Serve with the mayo spread.

PER SERVING: 404 calories, 20 g protein, 5 g carbohydrates, 35 g total fat, 4 g saturated fat, 4 g fiber, 437 mg sodium

SALMON BURGERS OVER PORTOBELLOS

PREP TIME: 10 MINUTES | TOTAL TIME: 20 MINUTES

Makes 4 servings

While these salmon burgers go well on portobello mushrooms, as in the recipe below, they can also be used as part of a sandwich between 2 slices of Basic Focaccia Flatbread (page 21) with Garlicky Mayo Spread (page 41). For a spicy version, add 1 seeded and finely chopped jalapeño pepper to the mixture and use cilantro in place of the dill.

4 large portobello mushrooms (4–5" diameter), stems removed

3 tablespoons melted coconut oil or extra-virgin olive oil, divided

¾ teaspoon sea salt, divided

2 scallions, finely chopped, or ¼ yellow onion, finely chopped

½ roasted red bell pepper, finely chopped

2 cans (6 ounces each) skinless and boneless pink salmon, drained and flaked

1 egg, lightly beaten

¼ cup ground golden flaxseeds

2 tablespoons chopped fresh dill

Preheat the oven to 400°F.

Brush the tops of the mushrooms with 1½ tablespoons of the oil and place, stem-side up, on a baking sheet. Drizzle ½ tablespoon of the oil over the gills, and sprinkle with ¼ teaspoon of the salt. Bake for 10 minutes.

Meanwhile, in a medium bowl, combine the scallions or onion, pepper, salmon, egg, flaxseeds, dill, and remaining ½ teaspoon salt. Mix well. Shape into 4 burgers.

In a medium skillet over medium heat, heat the remaining 1 tablespoon oil. Cook the burgers for 4 minutes, turning once, or until browned.

Place 1 burger on top of each mushroom. Bake for 5 minutes, or until heated through.

PER SERVING: 258 calories, 20 g protein, 7 g carbohydrates, 17 g total fat, 10 g saturated fat, 4 g fiber, 570 mg sodium

FISH TACOS WITH CHIPOTLE-AVOCADO CREAM

PREP TIME: 10 MINUTES | **TOTAL TIME:** 20 MINUTES

Makes 4 servings

Here's a light "taco" using lettuce leaves stuffed with a spicy avocado and fish filling. The Tortillas (page 29) or Flaxseed Wraps (page 26) can, of course, be used in place of the lettuce.

Chipotle peppers in adobo sauce are smoked ripe jalapeño peppers that are packed in a tomato-based sauce. They have a distinct smoky flavor and are typically found in the international section of supermarkets.

If you prefer a spicier sauce, additional Cajun Seasoning Mix can be added when it is blended; if you prefer a less spicy sauce, reduce the seasoning mix by half.

¼ cup butter, melted

2 canned chipotle peppers in adobo sauce, minced

3 tablespoons lime juice, divided

3 teaspoons freshly grated lime peel, divided

½ teaspoon sea salt, divided

1¼ pounds firm white fish, such as cod, halibut, or tilapia, cut into 4 pieces

½ cup sour cream

½ teaspoon seafood seasoning or Cajun Seasoning Mix (page 58)

1 ripe avocado, halved, pitted, and peeled

8 medium leaves lettuce (iceberg, romaine, or Bibb)

1½ cups finely shredded cabbage

Lime wedges (optional)

In a small bowl, combine the butter, peppers, 1 tablespoon of the lime juice, 2 teaspoons of the lime peel, and ¼ teaspoon of the salt until blended. Brush both sides of the fish fillets with the butter mixture. Lightly coat a grill pan or skillet with cooking spray and heat over medium-high heat. Cook the fish for 8 minutes, turning once, or until it flakes easily. Transfer to a plate and cover lightly with foil.

Meanwhile, in a blender or small food processor, combine the sour cream, seasoning mix, avocado, the remaining 2 tablespoons lime juice, the remaining 1 teaspoon lime peel, and the remaining ¼ teaspoon salt. Blend or process for 30 seconds, or until smooth. Place in a small bowl.

Flake the fish with a fork and place inside the lettuce leaves. Top with the chipotle-avocado cream and shredded cabbage. Serve with lime wedges, if desired.

PER SERVING: 384 calories, 28 g protein, 10 g carbohydrates, 27 g total fat, 13 g saturated fat, 4 g fiber, 428 mg sodium

CARIBBEAN SHRIMP AND RICE

PREP TIME: 10 MINUTES | **TOTAL TIME:** 25 MINUTES

Makes 4 servings

I use the Cajun Seasoning Mix in this quick and easy dish, but bring in the exotic Caribbean combination of ginger, cilantro, and lime.

½ large head cauliflower, broken into florets

2 tablespoons extra-virgin olive oil

4 scallions, sliced

1 red bell pepper, thinly sliced

1 can (14.5 ounces) diced tomatoes

1 teaspoon Cajun Seasoning Mix (page 58)

2 tablespoons grated fresh ginger or 2 teaspoons ground ginger

1 pound peeled and deveined medium shrimp, tails removed

Juice of 1 small lime

2 tablespoons coarsely chopped cilantro

Using a food processor with a shredding disk attachment or the largest holes of a box grater, shred the cauliflower. Place the shredded cauliflower in a microwaveable bowl. Cover and microwave on high power for 4 minutes, stirring once, or until desired doneness. Set aside.

In a large skillet over medium-high heat, heat the oil. Cook the scallions and pepper, stirring frequently, for 5 minutes, or until lightly browned. Stir in the tomatoes, seasoning mix, and ginger. Cook for 1 minute, or until simmering. Add the shrimp, cover, and cook for 3 minutes, or until the shrimp are opaque.

Stir in the reserved "riced" cauliflower, lime juice, and cilantro. Cook for 2 minutes or until heated through.

PER SERVING: 206 calories, 18 g protein, 14 g carbohydrates, 9 g total fat, 1 g saturated fat, 3 g fiber, 917 mg sodium

SHRIMP-STUFFED TOMATOES

PREP TIME: 15 MINUTES | **TOTAL TIME:** 15 MINUTES

Makes 4 servings

Lime and avocado mingle with the flavors of tomato to make an interesting way to enjoy shrimp. For fullest flavor, choose heirloom or beefsteak tomatoes, if available.

1 pound frozen cooked medium shrimp, thawed

6 large plum tomatoes, halved lengthwise

¼ cup Mayonnaise (page 40 or store-bought)

1 rib celery, finely chopped

2 scallions, thinly sliced

1 tablespoon lime juice

¼ teaspoon sea salt

1 large ripe avocado, halved, pitted, peeled, and chopped

Rinse the shrimp, pat completely dry with paper towels, and chop coarsely. Using a spoon, scoop out the flesh of each tomato half and discard.

In a medium bowl, whisk together the mayonnaise, celery, scallions, lime juice, and salt. Add the shrimp and toss to coat. Gently fold in the avocado. Divide the mixture among the tomatoes.

PER SERVING: 258 calories, 17 g protein, 9 g carbohydrates, 18 g total fat, 2 g saturated fat, 4 g fiber, 846 mg sodium

CREAMY SHRIMP MARINARA

PREP TIME: 5 MINUTES | TOTAL TIME: 25 MINUTES

Makes 4 servings

Humans were meant to eat shellfish!

Here's a way to enjoy shrimp that just about anybody can appreciate, kids on up. The shrimp go wonderfully with Zucchini Noodles, but shirataki noodles or "riced" cauliflower are other options. A dairy-free version can be made by replacing the heavy cream with canned coconut milk. For some added kick, sprinkle the finished dish with ½ teaspoon red-pepper flakes.

1 tablespoon extra-virgin olive oil

1 shallot, minced

3 cloves garlic, minced

1 can (28 ounces) crushed tomatoes

2 tablespoons tomato paste

1 teaspoon Italian Seasoning Mix (page 56)

1 pound peeled and deveined large shrimp, tails removed

½ cup heavy cream or canned coconut milk

Zucchini Noodles (page 130), optional

In a large skillet, heat the oil over medium heat. Cook the shallot and garlic for 2 minutes, stirring occasionally. Stir in the tomatoes, tomato paste, and seasoning mix and bring to a simmer. Reduce the heat to low and simmer for 10 minutes, stirring occasionally.

Add the shrimp, cover, and simmer for 3 minutes, or until opaque. Stir in the cream or coconut milk and cook for 2 minutes or until heated through. Serve over zucchini noodles, if desired.

PER SERVING: 293 calories, 20 g protein, 19 g carbohydrates, 16 g total fat, 8 g saturated fat, 4 g fiber, 981 mg sodium

CHORIZO-SHRIMP TORTILLAS

PREP TIME: 10 MINUTES | **TOTAL TIME:** 20 MINUTES

Makes 4 servings

The seemingly disparate spiciness of chorizo; the ocean flavors of shrimp; and the cool, fresh scent of cilantro come together deliciously in these easy tortillas.

This recipe's already quick, but you can save even more time by chopping the garlic and onion in the food processor. If you want to skip the tortillas altogether, add "riced" cauliflower when you add the shrimp to make an easy version of paella.

2 tablespoons extra-virgin olive oil

1 onion, finely chopped

2 cloves garlic, minced

6–8 ounces chorizo sausage, thinly sliced

1 pound peeled and deveined small to medium shrimp, tails removed

2 tablespoons Taco Seasoning Mix (page 57)

2 tablespoons chopped cilantro

4 Tortillas (page 29)

In a large skillet over medium heat, heat the oil. Cook the onion and garlic for 3 minutes, stirring constantly, or until softened.

Add the chorizo and cook for 5 minutes, stirring occasionally, or until cooked through. Add the shrimp and seasoning mix. Cook for 2 minutes, stirring frequently, or until opaque. Stir in the cilantro. Spoon over the tortillas.

PER SERVING: 405 calories, 29 g protein, 18 g carbohydrates, 26 g total fat, 4 g saturated fat, 8 g fiber, 998 mg sodium

INDIAN CURRY SHRIMP

PREP TIME: 5 MINUTES | **TOTAL TIME:** 15 MINUTES

Makes 4 servings

The fragrant and exotic scents of the curry in a thick coconut milk base create a wonderful way to enjoy seafood. To save even more time (and transform this into a Thai curry dish), skip the ginger, garlic, and curry powder and use 1 cup Thai Red Curry Sauce (page 36) in place of the coconut milk. Either way, try serving over "riced" cauliflower.

3 tablespoons coconut oil or ghee

1 onion, thinly sliced

1 teaspoon minced fresh ginger

1 teaspoon minced garlic

4 teaspoons curry powder

½ teaspoon sea salt

1 cup canned coconut milk

1½ pounds peeled and deveined medium shrimp, tails removed

2 tablespoons chopped cilantro

In a large skillet over medium heat, heat the oil or ghee. Cook the onion for 5 minutes, or until lightly browned. Stir in the ginger, garlic, curry powder, and salt and cook for 1 minute. Add the coconut milk and bring to a simmer. Add the shrimp and cook for 2 minutes, or until opaque. Remove from the heat and stir in the cilantro.

PER SERVING: 301 calories, 17 g protein, 7 g carbohydrates, 24 g total fat, 20 g saturated fat, 2 g fiber, 849 mg sodium

SHRIMP SCAMPI

PREP TIME: 10 MINUTES | **TOTAL TIME:** 20 MINUTES

Makes 4 servings

Classic shrimp scampi returns, free of the tyranny of the wheat noodle! While the shrimp scampi alone can be served alongside some steamed asparagus or fresh mushrooms sautéed in butter, serve it with shirataki noodles to mimic the classic Italian dish.

3 tablespoons extra-virgin olive oil, divided	1 teaspoon Italian Seasoning Mix (page 56)
3 ounces sliced fresh mushrooms (such as cremini)	3 tablespoons lemon juice
3 tablespoons butter, divided	2 tablespoons dry white wine or chicken broth
1½ pounds peeled and deveined large shrimp, tails removed	2 tablespoons minced fresh parsley
5 cloves garlic, minced	Cooked shirataki noodles (optional)

In a large skillet over medium-high heat, heat 1 tablespoon of the oil until hot. Cook the mushrooms for 5 minutes, stirring occasionally, or until lightly browned and their moisture is released. Transfer to a bowl and set aside.

Add the remaining 2 tablespoons oil and 1 tablespoon of the butter to the same skillet and heat over medium-high heat to melt the butter. Cook the shrimp for 2 minutes, stirring frequently, or just until opaque (do not overcook). Transfer to the bowl with the mushrooms.

Reduce the heat to medium. Melt 1 tablespoon of the butter in the skillet. Add the garlic and cook for 1 minute, stirring constantly. Add the remaining 1 tablespoon butter to the skillet along with the seasoning mix. Whisk in the lemon juice and wine or broth and cook for 1 minute, whisking constantly. Return the reserved shrimp and mushrooms, along with accumulated juices, to the skillet. Cook for 1 minute or until heated through. Stir in the parsley. Serve over shirataki noodles, if desired.

PER SERVING: 318 calories, 24 g protein, 5 g carbohydrates, 21 g total fat, 7 g saturated fat, 0.5 g fiber, 1,043 mg sodium

EASY BAKED SCALLOPS

PREP TIME: 10 MINUTES | **TOTAL TIME:** 25 MINUTES

Makes 4 servings

Here's a good, old-fashioned recipe for baked scallops dripping with butter, but with no sign of wheat! We replace bread crumbs with a mixture of almond meal/flour and Parmesan cheese that re-creates that buttery, crumbly topping that many wheat-free people miss.

¼ cup almond meal/flour

¼ cup finely grated Parmesan cheese

1 teaspoon seafood seasoning or Moroccan Seasoning Mix (page 48), divided

1 pound medium sea scallops, rinsed and patted dry

2 tablespoons lemon juice

2 tablespoons butter, melted

Preheat the oven to 375°F. Grease an 11" x 7" baking dish.

In a shallow bowl or dish, combine the almond meal/flour, cheese, and ½ teaspoon of the seasoning mix. Dredge the scallops in the cheese mixture, pressing to coat evenly. Place on the baking dish.

In a small bowl, combine the lemon juice, butter, and the remaining ½ teaspoon seasoning mix. Carefully drizzle over the scallops to keep the topping intact.

Bake for 12 minutes, or until just barely opaque. Turn the oven to broil and cook for 2 minutes, or until lightly browned on top.

PER SERVING: 197 calories, 17 g protein, 7 g carbohydrates, 12 g total fat, 5 g saturated fat, 1 g fiber, 677 mg sodium

CURRIED VEGETABLES

PREP TIME: 10 MINUTES | **TOTAL TIME:** 30 MINUTES

Makes 4 servings

These flavorful Indian curried vegetables can stand alone as a main dish or serve as a substantial side dish. The vegetables are easily varied; try using sliced carrots, baby onions, scallions, or broccoli.

2 tablespoons coconut oil

1 yellow onion, chopped

2 cloves garlic, minced

4 cups small frozen cauliflower florets, thawed, or fresh

2 cups frozen spinach, thawed, or 4 cups fresh spinach

1 large tomato, chopped

¾ cup Thai Red Curry Sauce (page 36)

¼ teaspoon sea salt

¼ cup coarsely chopped cilantro

In a large skillet over medium-high heat, heat the oil. Cook the onion and garlic for 3 minutes. Stir in the cauliflower, cover, and cook for 7 minutes, stirring occasionally. Add the spinach, tomato, curry sauce, and salt. Cover and simmer for 10 minutes, or until the cauliflower is soft. Stir in the cilantro.

PER SERVING: 311 calories, 5 g protein, 15 g carbohydrates, 28 g total fat, 24 g saturated fat, 5 g fiber, 493 mg sodium

SPANAKOPITA BURGERS

PREP TIME: 15 MINUTES | **TOTAL TIME:** 30 MINUTES

4 servings

This is a variation on spanakopita, or Greek spinach pie, that includes all of the wonderful flavorful ingredients—spinach, feta cheese, onion, and egg—but without the unhealthy effects of the crust. Here it is re-created as a burger that can be eaten as is or sandwiched between two slices of Sandwich Bread (page 20) or Basic Focaccia Flatbread (page 21).

3 tablespoons extra-virgin olive oil, divided

1 small yellow onion, finely chopped

2 packages (10 ounces each) frozen chopped spinach, thawed and squeezed dry

1 teaspoon dried oregano

½ teaspoon garlic salt

½ teaspoon ground black pepper

2 teaspoons fresh lemon juice

1 cup crumbled feta cheese

1 egg, lightly beaten

½ cup ground golden flaxseeds

In a large skillet over medium-high heat, heat 1 tablespoon of the oil. Cook the onion for 3 minutes, stirring frequently, or until lightly browned. Add the spinach and cook for 1 minute, stirring, or until heated through. Transfer to a medium bowl and allow to cool slightly. Add the oregano, garlic salt, pepper, lemon juice, cheese, egg, and flaxseeds. Mix to combine. Shape into 4 burgers.

In the skillet over medium heat, heat the remaining 2 tablespoons oil. Cook the burgers for 7 minutes, turning once, or until light brown.

PER SERVING: 322 calories, 12 g protein, 13 g carbohydrates, 24 g total fat, 7 g saturated fat, 6 g fiber, 670 mg sodium

KALE, ONION, AND GOAT CHEESE PIZZA

PREP TIME: 10 MINUTES | **TOTAL TIME:** 30 MINUTES

Makes 4 servings

The unique mix of flavors in this pizza, best suited to adult palates, elevates a casual dish to the level of something special!

PIZZA CRUST

- 2½ cups All-Purpose Baking Mix (page 19)
- ½ cup shredded mozzarella cheese
- ¼ teaspoon sea salt
- 1 egg
- 2 tablespoons extra-virgin olive oil
- ½ cup water

TOPPING

- 2 tablespoons extra-virgin olive oil
- 4 cups fresh or frozen kale, thawed, torn into small pieces
- 1 yellow onion, cut into wedges
- ¼ teaspoon sea salt
- ⅔ cup pizza sauce (no sugar added)
- 2 ounces goat cheese, crumbled

Preheat the oven to 400°F. Line a baking sheet or pizza pan with parchment paper.

To make the crust: In a medium bowl, combine the baking mix, cheese, and salt. In a small bowl, mix together the egg, oil, and water. Pour into the flour mixture and combine thoroughly.

Place the dough on the baking sheet or pizza pan and, with moistened hands, press into a 12" circle, forming an outer edge. Bake for 10 minutes. Remove from the oven and set aside. Reduce the heat to 350°F.

To make the topping: Meanwhile, in a large skillet over medium heat, heat the oil. Add the kale, onion, and salt and cook for 5 minutes, stirring frequently, or until the kale wilts and the onion is soft.

Top the pizza crust with the sauce, kale mixture, and goat cheese. Return to the oven for 10 minutes, or until the cheese melts.

PER SERVING: 698 calories, 27 g protein, 30 g carbohydrates, 57 g total fat, 9 g saturated fat, 14 g fiber, 1,015 mg sodium

PALAK PANEER

PREP TIME: 10 MINUTES | **TOTAL TIME:** 30 MINUTES

Makes 4 servings

This Indian/Pakistani dish serves up a walloping quantity of healthy spinach in an exotic curry sauce.

2 packages (6 ounces each) baby spinach

2 tablespoons ghee or coconut oil

12 ounces paneer cheese, cut into 1" cubes

1 onion, finely chopped

2 cloves garlic, minced

2 tablespoons Moroccan Seasoning Mix (page 48)

½ teaspoon sea salt

1 can (14.5 ounces) diced tomatoes or 1 tomato, chopped

½ cup canned coconut milk or cream

Place the spinach in a colander set in the sink. Carefully pour 4 cups boiling water over it to wilt the spinach. Set aside to drain.

In a large skillet over medium heat, heat the ghee or oil. Cook the cheese for 8 minutes, turning, or until browned. Remove from the skillet and set aside on a plate.

In the same skillet, cook the onion and garlic for 3 minutes, or until lightly browned. Add the seasoning mix and salt and stir for 1 minute. Add the reserved spinach, the tomatoes, and coconut milk or cream. Bring to a simmer. Reduce the heat to medium-low, cover, and simmer for 5 minutes.

Carefully pour the contents of the skillet into a food processor and process for 1 minute, or until the spinach and tomatoes are broken down and the mixture is creamy. Return to the skillet, add the reserved cheese, and heat through.

PER SERVING: 475 calories, 23 g protein, 20 g carbohydrates, 35 g total fat, 24 g saturated fat, 6 g fiber, 567 mg sodium

CHILES RELLENOS MINI CASSEROLES

PREP TIME: 5 MINUTES | **TOTAL TIME:** 30 MINUTES

Makes 4 servings

If you're in the mood for something Mexican besides a burrito, here's a nice little option that is deceptively filling and delicious.

If you wish, replace the salsa with a side of pico de gallo made with the ripest tomatoes.

4 eggs

¾ cup heavy cream or half-and-half

1 can (7 ounces) diced green chile peppers, drained

1½ cups shredded Cheddar or pepper Jack cheese, divided

4 tablespoons salsa (optional)

Preheat the oven to 400°F. Grease 4 (8- to 9-ounce) ramekins and place on a baking sheet.

In a medium bowl, whisk together the eggs and cream or half-and-half. Add the chile peppers and 1 cup of the cheese and whisk to combine. Divide evenly among the ramekins. Top with the remaining ½ cup cheese. Bake for 25 minutes, or until a knife inserted in the center comes out clean. Top each with 1 tablespoon salsa, if desired.

PER SERVING: 406 calories, 17 g protein, 5 g carbohydrates, 35 g total fat, 20 g saturated fat, 1 g fiber, 468 mg sodium

FETTUCCINE WITH BASIL-WALNUT PESTO

PREP TIME: 5 MINUTES | **TOTAL TIME:** 15 MINUTES

Makes 2 servings

Bring the magical combination of basil and extra-virgin olive oil together in this simple pasta dish.

Save time by using prepared basil pesto from the recipe on page 31 or store-bought.

1 cup packed fresh basil

¼ cup walnuts

3 cloves garlic, chopped

⅓ cup extra-virgin olive oil

¼ cup grated romano cheese

¼ teaspoon sea salt

2 teaspoons fresh lemon juice

2 packages (8 ounces each) shirataki fettuccine noodles, rinsed and drained

In a food chopper or food processor, combine the basil, walnuts, and garlic. Chop or process into a paste. Add the oil, cheese, salt, and lemon juice and chop or process until the mixture is blended and the pesto is bright green. Set aside.

Prepare the noodles according to package directions. Transfer to a serving bowl.

Top the noodles with the reserved basil mixture and toss to coat well.

PER SERVING: 498 calories, 9 g protein, 14 g carbohydrates, 48 g total fat, 7 g saturated fat, 8 g fiber, 403 mg sodium

SPAGHETTI WITH OLIVES, CAPERS, AND GARLIC

PREP TIME: 10 MINUTES | **TOTAL TIME:** 20 MINUTES

Makes 2 servings

This simple "pasta" dish can serve as a filling main course or a substantial side dish. Don't let the apparent small servings fool you: Remember that, minus the appetite-stimulating effects of the gliadin protein of wheat, appetites are satisfied with much less. And this pasta, unlike those made with conventional ingredients or the awful gluten-free flours, does not result in sky-high blood sugars or other distortions of metabolism.

¼ cup extra-virgin olive oil

3 cloves garlic, minced

3 scallions, sliced

¼ teaspoon sea salt

2 teaspoons capers

¼ cup pitted kalamata olives, sliced

2 packages (8 ounces each) shirataki noodles, rinsed and drained

¼ cup shredded Parmesan cheese

In a medium skillet over medium heat, heat the oil. Cook the garlic, scallions, and salt for 3 minutes, or until the scallions begin to soften. Stir in the capers and olives. Set aside.

Prepare the noodles according to package directions. Transfer to a serving bowl. Top with the reserved olive mixture and toss to coat. Sprinkle with the cheese.

PER SERVING: 425 calories, 5 g protein, 9 g carbohydrates, 41 g total fat, 7 g saturated fat, 1 g fiber, 1,142 mg sodium

JAPANESE EGGPLANT STIR-FRY

PREP TIME: 15 MINUTES | TOTAL TIME: 30 MINUTES

Makes 4 servings

I've served this Japanese eggplant as both a main dish and a substantial side dish alongside beef that had been marinated and sautéed in a (gluten-free) teriyaki sauce. Optionally, a pound of finely sliced beef or pork or shrimp can be combined with the eggplant itself. (Meat or shrimp should be cooked separately, then combined.) If noodles are desired, shirataki would be perfect. Japanese eggplants can be found in most Asian grocery stores and in some specialty supermarkets.

3 tablespoons sesame oil, divided

1½ pounds Japanese eggplants, quartered lengthwise and sliced ½" thick

6 scallions, sliced

4 cloves garlic, minced

3 tablespoons gluten-free soy sauce

2 tablespoons grated fresh ginger

¼ cup water

½ cup coarsely chopped cilantro

2 teaspoons sesame seeds

In a large skillet over medium heat, heat 2 tablespoons of the oil. Add the eggplant, cover, and cook for 10 minutes, stirring occasionally, or until softened.

Add the remaining 1 tablespoon oil. Stir in the scallions, garlic, soy sauce, ginger, and water. Cover and simmer for 5 minutes, stirring occasionally, or until the eggplant is completely soft. Just before serving, stir in the cilantro and sprinkle with the sesame seeds.

PER SERVING: 160 calories, 4 g protein, 14 g carbohydrates, 11 g total fat, 1.5 g saturated fat, 5 g fiber, 669 mg sodium

BROCCOLI-CHEESE CASSEROLE

PREP TIME: 10 MINUTES | **TOTAL TIME:** 30 MINUTES

Makes 4 servings

This simple casserole can serve as either a main dish or a substantial side dish along-side pork chops, baked chicken, or any form of beef. Other vegetables, such as fresh asparagus or green beans, can be added or can replace the broccoli. A can of baby onions can also be added for a little extra zing.

1 bag (12 ounces) fresh broccoli florets

½ cup water

2 eggs

1 cup shredded sharp Cheddar cheese, divided

½ cup heavy cream

⅓ cup almond meal/flour

½ teaspoon mustard powder

¼ teaspoon onion powder

¼ teaspoon sea salt

Dash of ground red pepper (optional)

Preheat the oven to 400°F. Grease an 8" x 8" baking dish.

In a microwaveable bowl, place the broccoli florets and water, cover, and microwave on high power for 3 minutes, or until the broccoli is bright green and softened. Drain and place in the baking dish.

In a medium bowl, combine the eggs, ½ cup of the cheese, the cream, almond meal/flour, mustard, onion powder, salt, and red pepper (if desired). Pour over the broccoli. Top with the remaining ½ cup cheese.

Bake for 20 minutes, or until a knife inserted in the center comes out clean.

PER SERVING: 332 calories, 15 g protein, 8 g carbohydrates, 28 g total fat, 14 g saturated fat, 4 g fiber, 249 mg sodium

DESSERTS AND SNACKS

COCONUT-CHOCOLATE TART

PREP TIME: 5 MINUTES | **TOTAL TIME:** 20 MINUTES + CHILLING TIME

Makes 8 servings

Shredded coconut makes a sturdy and delicious piecrust. Here I fill a coconut crust with a rich chocolate cream to make a delightful tart appropriate for celebrations, holidays, or an extra-special dessert.

1¾ cups + 2 tablespoons shredded unsweetened coconut

3 tablespoons All-Purpose Baking Mix (page 19)

Sweetener equivalent to 3 tablespoons + ½ cup sugar

3 tablespoons coconut oil or butter, melted

14 ounces canned coconut milk

8 ounces unsweetened chocolate, chopped

½ teaspoon vanilla extract

¼ teaspoon almond extract

Preheat the oven to 350°F. Grease a 9" pie plate.

In a medium bowl, combine the coconut, baking mix, sweetener equivalent to 3 tablespoons of sugar, and the oil or butter and mix thoroughly. Press into the pie plate and bake for 10 minutes, or until the edges are lightly browned. Remove and cool.

Meanwhile, in a medium saucepan over medium-high heat, heat the coconut milk just until bubbles begin to form. Remove from the heat, add the chocolate, and stir until melted. Stir in the vanilla, almond extract, and the remaining sweetener equivalent to ½ cup sugar until blended. Pour into the coconut shell. Refrigerate until set, at least 1 hour.

PER SERVING: 453 calories, 7 g protein, 14 g carbohydrates, 46 g total fat, 36 g saturated fat, 8 g fiber, 28 mg sodium

KID-FRIENDLY

BERRY-COCONUT MINI CHEESECAKES

PREP TIME: 10 MINUTES | **TOTAL TIME:** 30 MINUTES + COOLING TIME

Makes 12 cakes

All doubts over how delicious a wheat-free lifestyle can be will crumble with these delicious mini cheesecakes!

I top these with fresh berries, but you can substitute with a drizzle of dark chocolate, a sprinkle of cocoa powder, or some more shredded coconut.

1¼ cups All-Purpose Baking Mix (page 19)

Sweetener equivalent to 1 tablespoon + ½ cup sugar

3 tablespoons coconut oil or butter, melted

12 ounces cream cheese, at room temperature

½ cup sour cream or plain Greek yogurt

2 eggs

¼ cup shredded unsweetened coconut

1½ cups fresh mixed berries

Preheat the oven to 350°F. Place paper liners in a 12-cup muffin pan.

In a large bowl, combine the baking mix, sweetener equivalent to 1 tablespoon sugar, and the coconut oil or butter. Mix thoroughly. Divide among the muffin cups. Press flat in the bottom of each cup with a spoon or your fingers. Set aside.

In a large bowl, with an electric mixer, blend the cream cheese and the remaining sweetener equivalent to ½ cup sugar until smooth. Stir in the sour cream or yogurt. Add the eggs, one at a time, mixing until thoroughly incorporated. Stir in the coconut and mix thoroughly. Divide the batter among the muffin cups. Bake for 20 minutes, or until a knife inserted in the center comes out clean. (The cheesecakes will puff up during baking and then fall as they cool.)

Allow to cool in the muffin pan for 5 minutes. Remove to a rack to cool completely. Serve each topped with 2 tablespoons of berries.

PER CHEESECAKE: 265 calories, 6 g protein, 16 g carbohydrates, 22 g total fat, 11 g saturated fat, 3 g fiber, 166 mg sodium

CINNAMON DONUTS

PREP TIME: 10 MINUTES | **TOTAL TIME:** 20 MINUTES + COOLING TIME

Makes 12 donuts

An unusual technique is used to create these mini-donuts. The result: delicious, bite-size, *healthy* snacks! Because these donuts, unlike conventional wheat flour/sugary/fried donuts, are without adverse health implications, you can have them for breakfast, snacks, or dessert without worry.

Optionally, you can drizzle the Chocolate Glaze (page 214) or Vanilla Glaze (page 215) over the top.

¼ cup ground golden flaxseeds	1½ teaspoons ground cinnamon
1 cup cold water	½ teaspoon baking soda
¾ cup coconut flour	½ cup coconut oil, melted
¾ cup shredded unsweetened coconut	1 egg
Sweetener equivalent to ½ cup sugar	

Preheat the oven to 375°F. Grease a donut pan.

In a small mug or bowl, stir together the flaxseeds and water, then place it in the freezer for 5 minutes.

In a large bowl, combine the coconut flour, coconut, sweetener, cinnamon, and baking soda, and mix. Stir in the coconut oil until well mixed.

Remove the flaxseeds from the freezer and whisk in the egg. Pour the flaxseed mixture into the coconut mixture and mix. Spoon the mixture into the donut pan, pressing into wells, if necessary.

Bake for 10 minutes, or until the donuts are slightly firm to the touch and the edges are golden. Allow to cool in the pan for 5 minutes before inverting onto a wire rack to cool completely.

PER DONUT: 189 calories, 2 g protein, 15 g carbohydrates, 15 g total fat, 12 g saturated fat, 5 g fiber, 61 mg sodium

MINI CHOCOLATE ÉCLAIRS

PREP TIME: 10 MINUTES | **TOTAL TIME:** 30 MINUTES + COOLING TIME

Makes 8 éclairs

Yes: chocolate éclairs! But these are actually healthy. For a more luxurious topping, try the Chocolate Glaze on page 214.

½ cup canned coconut milk, well stirred

¼ cup butter

¼ cup coconut flour

2 teaspoons ground psyllium seeds

⅛ teaspoon sea salt

2 eggs, at room temperature

8 ounces heavy cream

Sweetener equivalent to 2 tablespoons sugar

½ teaspoon vanilla extract

1 bar (3.5 ounces) dark chocolate (70–86% cocoa), chopped and melted

Preheat the oven to 375°F. Line a baking sheet with parchment paper.

In a medium saucepan over medium heat, bring the coconut milk and butter to a boil. Remove from the heat and add the flour, psyllium seeds, and salt all at once. Stir until incorporated. Return the saucepan to the heat and stir until the mixture pulls together into a loose ball. Remove from the heat and continue stirring for 1 minute, to cool the mixture slightly. Add the eggs, one at a time, stirring to thoroughly incorporate. Stir until the mixture is mostly smooth and takes on a slight sheen.

Spoon or pipe the mixture into eight 2" to 3" lines on the baking sheet. Bake for 20 minutes, or until golden and slightly firm. Remove to a wire rack to cool completely.

Meanwhile, in a large bowl, with an electric mixer on high speed, beat the cream until stiff peaks form. With the mixer on low speed, blend in the sweetener and vanilla. Set aside.

Slice each éclair puff in half, and remove the center dough. Dollop the whipped cream mixture onto the bottom halves. Replace the tops. Drizzle the chocolate over the tops.

PER 1 ÉCLAIR: 280 calories, 4 g protein, 10 g carbohydrates, 26 g total fat, 17 g saturated fat, 4 g fiber, 116 mg sodium

DOUBLE CHOCOLATE MINI CAKES

PREP TIME: 5 MINUTES | **TOTAL TIME:** 30 MINUTES

Makes 4 cakes

Kids love having their own little cakes. These 3" mini cakes are just the right size for a filling and healthy celebration.

If a fine cake texture is desired, substitute the baking mix with almond flour from blanched almonds. Optionally, Chocolate Glaze (page 214) or Chocolate Frosting (page 217) can be added for *triple* chocolate mini cakes.

1¼ cups All-Purpose Baking Mix (page 19)

2 tablespoons unsweetened cocoa powder

Sweetener equivalent to ¾ cup sugar

⅓ cup dark chocolate chips

1 teaspoon white vinegar

6 tablespoons coconut milk (canned or carton), milk, or half-and-half

½ tablespoon molasses

1 egg, beaten

Preheat the oven to 375°F. Grease four 4-ounce ramekins.

In a large bowl, combine the baking mix, cocoa, sweetener, and chocolate chips. Mix well.

Stir in the vinegar and coconut milk, milk, or half-and-half. Allow to stand for 1 minute. Stir in the molasses and egg, mixing thoroughly. The batter should be the consistency of conventional cake batter, but if it's too thick, add more coconut milk, milk, or half-and-half, 1 tablespoon at a time, until the desired thickness is achieved.

Divide the batter among the ramekins. Arrange on a baking sheet and bake for 25 minutes, or until a wooden pick inserted in the center of a cake comes out clean.

PER CAKE: 371 calories, 12 g protein, 21 g carbohydrates, 30 g total fat, 10 g saturated fat, 9 g fiber, 195 mg sodium

MOROCCAN CHICKEN WITH ROASTED BELL PEPPERS | 156

COCONUT-CHOCOLATE TART | 194

KEY LIME CUPCAKES

PREP TIME: 5 MINUTES | **TOTAL TIME:** 25 MINUTES + COOLING TIME

Makes 12 cupcakes

If your kids love the sharper, tart flavor of Key limes like mine do, then these Key Lime Cupcakes are sure to satisfy! Modify the tartness simply by increasing or decreasing the amount of lime juice. For an extra-light cake texture, substitute the baking mix with almond flour from blanched almonds.

CUPCAKES

- 4 cups All-Purpose Baking Mix (page 19)
- Sweetener equivalent to 1 cup sugar
- ½ teaspoon sea salt
- 1 cup Key lime juice
- 3 eggs

FROSTING

- 8 ounces cream cheese, at room temperature
- Sweetener equivalent to ½ cup sugar
- 2 teaspoons Key lime juice

Preheat the oven to 350°F. Place paper liners in a 12-cup muffin pan.

To make the cupcakes: In a large bowl, combine the baking mix, sweetener, and salt. Mix well. Stir in the lime juice and allow to stand for 1 minute. Whisk the eggs and stir into the mixture.

Divide the batter among the muffin cups. Bake for 20 minutes, or until a wooden pick inserted in the center of a cupcake comes out clean.

To make the frosting: In a small bowl, combine the cream cheese, sweetener, and lime juice. Mix well. Spread over the tops of the cooled cupcakes.

PER CUPCAKE: 299 calories, 11 g protein, 13 g carbohydrates, 25 g total fat, 5 g saturated fat, 6 g fiber, 350 mg sodium

PISTACHIO-GREEN TEA CUPCAKES

PREP TIME: 10 MINUTES | **TOTAL TIME:** 30 MINUTES + COOLING TIME

Makes 12 cupcakes

If you love green tea and the health benefits it provides, the ground powder from green tea leaves is a little-known way to obtain them. The green tea powder can be purchased already ground, usually from the matcha variety, or it can be ground from dried green tea leaves.

CUPCAKES

- 4 cups All-Purpose Baking Mix (page 19)
- Sweetener equivalent to 1 cup sugar
- ¾ cup raw pistachios, finely chopped
- ½ teaspoon sea salt
- 2 teaspoons lemon juice or white vinegar
- 1 cup buttermilk
- ¼ cup coconut oil, melted
- 3 eggs

FROSTING

- 8 ounces cream cheese, at room temperature
- Sweetener equivalent to ½ cup sugar
- 2 teaspoons green tea powder
- ½ teaspoon ground cardamom

Preheat the oven to 350°F. Place paper liners in a 12-cup muffin pan.

To make the cupcakes: In a large bowl, combine the baking mix, sweetener, pistachios, and salt. Stir in the lemon juice or vinegar and allow to stand for 1 minute. In a separate bowl, combine the buttermilk, oil, and eggs. Stir into the flour mixture.

Divide the batter among the muffin cups. Bake for 20 minutes, or until a wooden pick inserted in the center of a cupcake comes out clean.

To make the frosting: In a small bowl, combine the cream cheese, sweetener, green tea, and cardamom. Mix well. Spread over the tops of the cooled cupcakes.

PER CUPCAKE: 322 calories, 12 g protein, 13 g carbohydrates, 27 g total fat, 6 g saturated fat, 7 g fiber, 320 mg sodium

TART TANGERINE CUPCAKES

PREP TIME: 5 MINUTES | **TOTAL TIME:** 25 MINUTES + COOLING TIME

Makes 12 cupcakes

When in season, tangerines can be used to make a wonderfully flavorful, tart cupcake with the wheat-free baking mix. If tangerines are unavailable, you can make these orangey cupcakes with larger minneola tangerines, Mandarin oranges (though 3 or 4 will be required), or navel oranges.

CUPCAKES

- 4 cups All-Purpose Baking Mix (page 19)
- Sweetener equivalent to 1 cup sugar
- ½ teaspoon sea salt
- 1 cup tangerine juice or orange juice
- 3 eggs

FROSTING

- 8 ounces cream cheese, at room temperature
- Sweetener equivalent to ½ cup sugar
- 2 teaspoons tangerine juice or orange juice

Preheat the oven to 350°F. Place paper liners in a 12-cup muffin pan.

To make the cupcakes: In a large bowl, combine the baking mix, sweetener, and salt. Mix well. In a cup, reserve 2 teaspoons of the juice for the frosting. Add the remaining juice to the dry ingredients and stir well. Allow to stand for 1 to 2 minutes. Whisk the eggs and stir into the mixture.

Divide the batter among the muffin cups. Bake for 20 minutes, or until a wooden pick inserted in the center of a cupcake comes out clean.

To make the frosting: In a small bowl, combine the cream cheese, sweetener, and the reserved 2 teaspoons juice. Mix well. Spread over the tops of the cooled cupcakes.

PER CUPCAKE: 303 calories, 11 g protein, 13 g carbohydrates, 25 g total fat, 5 g saturated fat, 6 g fiber, 327 mg sodium

MACADAMIA-SPICE MUFFINS

PREP TIME: 5 MINUTES | TOTAL TIME: 30 MINUTES

Makes 12 muffins

Macadamia nuts join cinnamon and nutmeg in this healthy and filling muffin. Remember: In this wheat-free lifestyle, unhealthy ingredients are eliminated—fat is *not* one of them. So enjoy your reacquaintance with high-fat macadamia nuts!

4 cups All-Purpose Baking Mix (page 19)

1½ teaspoons baking soda

Sweetener equivalent to 1½ cups sugar

¾ cup chopped macadamia nuts

1 teaspoon ground cinnamon

½ teaspoon ground nutmeg

½ teaspoon sea salt

1 tablespoon lemon juice or vinegar

½ cup water

2 tablespoons molasses

3 eggs

Preheat the oven to 350°F. Grease a 12-cup muffin pan.

In a large bowl, combine the baking mix, baking soda, sweetener, nuts, cinnamon, nutmeg, and salt. Mix well.

In a small bowl, combine the lemon juice or vinegar, water, and molasses and mix. Add to the dry mixture and mix thoroughly.

In a small bowl, whisk the eggs. Add to the batter and mix thoroughly.

Divide the batter among the prepared muffin cups. Bake for 25 minutes, or until a wooden pick inserted in the center of a muffin comes out clean.

PER MUFFIN: 299 calories, 11 g protein, 14 g carbohydrates, 25 g total fat, 3 g saturated fat, 7 g fiber, 425 mg sodium

APPLE STREUSEL MUFFINS

PREP TIME: 10 MINUTES | **TOTAL TIME:** 30 MINUTES

Makes 12 muffins

If you like coffee cake with crumbly streusel topping, here's a little nostalgia for you—with none of the heartache!

The streusel topping works with any sweetener, but xylitol works the best, as it creates the sturdiest and most crumbly end result.

4 cups All-Purpose Baking Mix (page 19)

Sweetener equivalent to ½ cup sugar

1 teaspoon ground cinnamon

¼ teaspoon ground nutmeg

½ teaspoon sea salt

1 cup unsweetened applesauce

3 eggs

1 tablespoon molasses

½ cup butter, cut into small pieces

Preheat the oven to 325°F. Place paper liners in a 12-cup muffin pan.

In a large bowl, combine the baking mix, sweetener, cinnamon, nutmeg, and salt. Mix well. Set aside 1 cup of the mixture in a medium bowl. In a small bowl, combine the applesauce and eggs and stir until smooth. Add to the dry mixture and stir to combine. Divide the batter among the muffin cups.

To make the streusel topping, add the molasses to the reserved dry mixture. Cut in the butter until the mixture becomes crumbly. Spoon gently over the tops of the muffins. Bake for 20 minutes, or until a wooden pick inserted in the center of a muffin comes out clean.

PER MUFFIN: 311 calories, 10 g protein, 14 g carbohydrates, 27 g total fat, 7 g saturated fat, 7 g fiber, 334 mg sodium

APPLE PIE WHOOPIES

PREP TIME: 10 MINUTES | TOTAL TIME: 20 MINUTES + COOLING TIME

Makes 10 whoopies

As the name suggests, these little whoopies taste like a slice of apple pie. The kids will think it's dessert, but it's every bit as healthy as eating some nuts and apples!

CAKES

- 2 cups All-Purpose Baking Mix (page 19)
- ¾ cup finely chopped walnuts
- ¼ teaspoon ground ginger or ground cardamom
- Sweetener equivalent to ½ cup sugar
- ½ cup unsweetened chunky applesauce
- 2 teaspoons lemon juice
- 1 egg, whisked

GLAZE

- 2 tablespoons xylitol
- 2 ounces cream cheese
- ½ teaspoon lemon juice

Preheat the oven to 350°F. Grease 10 cups of a whoopie baking pan.*

To make the cakes: In a large bowl, combine the baking mix, walnuts, ginger or cardamom, and sweetener. Mix in the applesauce, lemon juice, and egg until thoroughly combined.

Divide the batter among the whoopie cups. Bake for 10 minutes, or until slightly firm and golden. Allow to cool in the pan for 5 minutes. Invert onto a rack to cool completely.

To make the glaze: Meanwhile, in a small microwaveable bowl, combine the xylitol and cream cheese. Microwave on high power in 10-second increments until melted. Mix thoroughly. Add the lemon juice and stir to combine.

When the cakes have cooled, drizzle them with the glaze.

PER WHOOPIE: 218 calories, 7 g protein, 9 g carbohydrates, 19 g total fat, 3 g saturated fat, 5 g fiber, 135 mg sodium

*Note: Baking your wheat-free dough in the shallow cups of a whoopie pan provides easy and consistent baked final products. If you don't have a whoopie pan, these pies are easy to form with your hands. Just divide the dough into 2-ounce portions, then create 3" patties and bake on a baking sheet lined with parchment paper.

CINNAMON ROLL WHOOPIES

PREP TIME: 10 MINUTES | **TOTAL TIME:** 20 MINUTES + COOLING TIME

Makes 10 whoopies

To make these whoopies seem even more like cinnamon rolls, you can add ¼ cup chopped pecans or chopped walnuts to the batter, or sprinkle the nuts on top of the glaze.

Serve these Cinnamon Roll Whoopies hot, topped with either the glaze or a pat of butter.

CAKES

- 2 **cups All-Purpose Baking Mix (page 19)**
- 2 **teaspoons ground cinnamon**
  Sweetener equivalent to ½ cup sugar
- 1 **teaspoon vanilla extract**
- ½ **cup heavy cream**

- 2 **teaspoons lemon juice**
- 1 **egg, whisked**

GLAZE

- 2 **tablespoons xylitol**
- 2 **ounces cream cheese**
- ½ **teaspoon lemon juice**

Preheat the oven to 350°F. Grease 10 cups of a whoopie baking pan.*

To make the cakes: In a large bowl, combine the baking mix, cinnamon, and sweetener. Mix in the vanilla, cream, lemon juice, and egg until thoroughly combined.

Divide the batter among the whoopie cups. Bake for 10 minutes, or until slightly firm and golden. Allow to cool in the pan for 5 minutes before inverting onto a rack.

To make the glaze: Meanwhile, in a small microwaveable bowl, combine the xylitol and cream cheese. Microwave on high power in 10-second increments until melted. Mix thoroughly. Add the lemon juice and stir to combine.

Drizzle the cakes with the glaze.

PER WHOOPIE: 188 calories, 6 g protein, 7 g carbohydrates, 16 g total fat, 4 g saturated fat, 4 g fiber, 130 mg sodium

* See note on opposite page.

PLUM JAM WHOOPIES

PREP TIME: 10 MINUTES | **TOTAL TIME:** 25 MINUTES + COOLING TIME

Makes 10 whoopies

Think of this recipe whenever you've made a batch of Plum-Chia Jam. It's a great way to make use of the leftovers!

CAKES

2 cups All-Purpose Baking Mix (page 19)

Sweetener equivalent to ½ cup sugar

½ cup + 2 tablespoons Plum-Chia Jam (page 51)

¼ cup water

1 teaspoon lemon juice

1 egg, whisked

GLAZE

2 tablespoons xylitol

2 ounces cream cheese

½ teaspoon lemon juice

....

Preheat the oven to 350°F. Grease 10 cups of a whoopie baking pan.

To make the cakes: In a large bowl, combine the baking mix and sweetener. Mix in ½ cup of the jam, the water, lemon juice, and egg until thoroughly combined.

Divide the batter among the 10 whoopie cups. Bake for 15 minutes, or until slightly firm and golden. Allow to cool in the pan for 5 minutes. Invert onto a rack to cool completely.

To make the glaze: Meanwhile, in a small microwaveable bowl, combine the xylitol and cream cheese. Microwave on high power in 10-second increments until melted. Mix thoroughly. Add the lemon juice and stir to combine.

Drizzle the cakes with the glaze. Spoon a small dollop of the remaining 2 tablespoons jam on top of the glaze.

PER WHOOPIE: 167 calories, 6 g protein, 9 g carbohydrates, 13 g total fat, 2 g saturated fat, 4 g fiber, 135 mg sodium

* See note on page 204.

BERRY FOOL

PREP TIME: 5 MINUTES | **TOTAL TIME:** 5 MINUTES

Makes 4 servings

Three simple ingredients combine for a delicious treat that comes together in minutes.

1 cup fresh berries of choice
Sweetener equivalent to
2 tablespoons sugar

1 cup heavy cream

In a food processor, pulse the berries with the sweetener until crushed, about 10 pulses. In a large bowl, with an electric mixer on high speed, beat the cream until stiff peaks form. Gently fold in the berries. Spoon into serving glasses and serve immediately or chill to serve later.

PER SERVING: 223 calories, 2 g protein, 5 g carbohydrates, 22 g total fat, 14 g saturated fat, 2 g fiber, 23 mg sodium

MOCHA KEFIRS

PREP TIME: 1 MINUTE | **TOTAL TIME:** 2 MINUTES

Makes 2 servings

If you haven't had kefir, you are in for a real treat. This is like eating melted ice cream!

2 cups kefir

Sweetener equivalent to
¼ cup sugar

1 teaspoon instant coffee granules

1 tablespoon unsweetened
cocoa powder

In a blender, combine the kefir, sweetener, coffee granules, and cocoa. Blend at medium speed until thick.

PER SERVING: 120 calories, 11 g protein, 14 g carbohydrates, 2 g total fat, 1 g saturated fat, 1 g fiber, 123 mg sodium

STRAWBERRY KEFIRS

PREP TIME: 1 MINUTE | **TOTAL TIME:** 2 MINUTES

Makes 2 servings

This kefir is a hit with kids. It can easily be altered to create blueberry, blackberry, or mixed berry kefirs too.

2 **cups kefir**
Sweetener equivalent to ¼ cup sugar

½ **cup fresh or frozen strawberries**
2 **mint sprigs, for garnish (optional)**

In a blender, combine the kefir, sweetener, and strawberries. Blend at medium speed until thick.

Serve as is or garnished with mint sprigs, if desired.

PER SERVING: 122 calories, 11 g protein, 15 g carbohydrates, 2 g total fat, 1 g saturated fat, 1 g fiber, 124 mg sodium

LEMON MOUSSE

Makes 6 servings

This quick, light dessert takes only 15 minutes to whip up but yields a wonderfully thick, rich mousse. I like serving it topped with fresh raspberries.

1 cup heavy cream

4 ounces cream cheese, at room temperature

Grated peel and juice of 1 lemon

Sweetener equivalent to 1 tablespoon sugar

1 teaspoon vanilla extract

In a large bowl, with an electric mixer on high speed, beat the cream until stiff peaks form. Set aside.

In a separate bowl, with the same mixer at medium speed, beat the cream cheese, lemon peel and juice, sweetener, and vanilla until blended. Gently fold the reserved whipped cream into the cream cheese mixture until thoroughly combined. Serve immediately or chill to serve later.

PER SERVING: 199 calories, 2 g protein, 3 g carbohydrates, 20 g total fat, 12 g saturated fat, 0 g fiber, 75 mg sodium

VANILLA CUSTARD

PREP TIME: 5 MINUTES | **TOTAL TIME:** 15 MINUTES + CHILLING TIME

Makes 4 servings

In the age of processed foods, many people have forgotten the simple art of making custard. Here is the basic recipe that can serve as the basis for a wide variety of rich custards, just by adding fresh or frozen berries, some unsweetened cocoa powder and dark chocolate chips, or chopped nuts. (You can also take the finished, cooled custard and process it in an ice cream maker according to the manufacturer's directions. Also note that the addition of the custard step allows the use of coconut milk in place of dairy cream while maintaining a thick texture and smooth mouthfeel, a perennial struggle with dairy-free ice custards.)

1½ **cups heavy cream or canned coconut milk**

4 **egg yolks**

Sweetener equivalent to ½ cup sugar

¼ **teaspoon sea salt**

1 **teaspoon vanilla extract**

1 **tablespoon butter, at room temperature**

In a medium saucepan over medium-high heat, heat the cream or coconut milk for 5 minutes, stirring with a wooden spoon, or just until bubbles start to form around the edges. Meanwhile, in a medium bowl, whisk together the egg yolks, sweetener, salt, and vanilla. Gradually whisk the hot cream or coconut milk into the yolk mixture until blended.

Pour back into the saucepan. Cook over medium heat for 5 minutes, stirring constantly, or until the mixture thickens. Remove from the heat and whisk in the butter until thoroughly incorporated and the custard is smooth.

Pour into a clean bowl and place plastic wrap directly on the surface to prevent a skin from forming. Chill until ready to serve.

PER SERVING: 394 calories, 5 g protein, 3 g carbohydrates, 41 g total fat, 24 g saturated fat, 0 g fiber, 166 mg sodium

CARAMEL SAUCE

PREP TIME: 5 MINUTES | **TOTAL TIME:** 15 MINUTES

Makes ¾ cup

This recipe is similar to the Vanilla Glaze (page 215), just cooked a bit longer to create the deep flavor and golden brown color of caramel. Serve this caramel sauce on top of Vanilla Custard (page 211), drizzled on Cinnamon Doughnuts (page 196), or over Apple Streusel Muffins (page 203).

¼ **cup butter**

⅓ **cup xylitol**

¼ **cup heavy cream**

½ **teaspoon vanilla extract**

In a small saucepan over medium-high heat, combine the butter and xylitol. Mix well, then stop stirring as it heats. Allow the butter to brown and the xylitol to melt, occasionally gently swirling the saucepan, for 5 minutes.

Remove the saucepan from the heat. In a measuring cup or small bowl, combine the cream and vanilla. Stir, 1 tablespoon at a time, into the butter mixture. Be careful, as the mixture will bubble up and may spurt. Continue adding the cream mixture and stirring until incorporated. Allow the sauce to cool for 5 minutes before serving.

PER 1 TABLESPOON: 53 calories, 0 g protein, 1 g carbohydrates, 6 g total fat, 3 g saturated fat, 0 g fiber, 6 mg sodium

LEMON WHIPPED CREAM

PREP TIME: 5 MINUTES | **TOTAL TIME:** 5 MINUTES

Makes 1½ cups

Serve this flavorful cream with a few berries for a last-minute delicious dessert.

1 cup heavy cream

1 teaspoon grated lemon peel

1 tablespoon lemon juice

In a large bowl, with an electric mixer on high speed, beat the cream until stiff peaks form. Gently stir in the lemon peel and juice. Use immediately or chill, covered, for up to 1 day.

PER 1 TABLESPOON: 35 calories, 0 g protein, 0 g carbohydrates, 4 g total fat, 2 g saturated fat, 0 g fiber, 4 mg sodium

CHOCOLATE GLAZE

PREP TIME: 5 MINUTES | TOTAL TIME: 10 MINUTES + COOLING TIME

Makes 1¼ cups

Drizzle this glaze over cookies, cupcakes, or muffins. For a dairy-free version, substitute coconut milk for the cream. Increase or decrease the quantity of cream to thin or thicken the glaze.

2 **bars (3.5 ounces each) dark chocolate (85–86% cocoa), chopped**

2 **tablespoons butter, softened**
½ **cup heavy cream**

In the top of a double boiler, place the chocolate over simmering water and stir until melted. Remove from the heat and stir in the butter until melted. Stir in the cream until smooth and well combined. Allow to cool for several minutes before dipping or coating.

PER 1 TABLESPOON: 80 calories, 1 g protein, 5 g carbohydrates, 8 g total fat, 4 g saturated fat, 1 g fiber, 12 mg sodium

VANILLA GLAZE

PREP TIME: 5 MINUTES | **TOTAL TIME:** 5 MINUTES + COOLING TIME

Makes ⅓ cup

This glaze achieves a caramel-like texture due to the unique properties of xylitol, the sugar replacement that most behaves like sugar in baking.

¼ cup heavy cream

½ teaspoon vanilla extract

¼ cup xylitol

1 tablespoon butter

In a small saucepan over low heat, heat the cream, vanilla, and xylitol until frothy, stirring constantly. Cook for 1 to 2 minutes, stirring constantly, or until bubbles form around the side of the saucepan. Do not scorch. Remove from the heat. Stir in the butter until smooth. Allow to cool to achieve desired thickness before drizzling, dipping, or coating.

PER 1 TABLESPOON: 20 calories, 0 g protein, 0 g carbohydrates, 2 g total fat, 1 g saturated fat, 0 g fiber, 8 mg sodium

STRAWBERRY GLAZE

PREP TIME: 5 MINUTES | **TOTAL TIME:** 15 MINUTES + COOLING TIME

Makes 1½ cups

This simple glaze makes a syrupy topping for ice cream or custard, pancakes, or Breakfast Cheesecake (page 74).

Note that xylitol was chosen as the sweetener in this recipe because of its unique glazing properties. Other sweeteners, such as stevia and erythritol, should not be substituted, as they will not yield the glaze effect.

4 cups fresh strawberries, hulled and quartered

4 tablespoons xylitol

In a food chopper, food processor, or blender, pulse the strawberries and xylitol until pureed.

In a medium saucepan over medium heat, heat the strawberry mixture. Allow to bubble and froth. Reduce the heat to low.

Cook for 5 minutes, stirring frequently, or until the mixture thickens and becomes syrupy. Be careful not to let the mixture boil or burn. Remove from the heat and allow to cool.

PER 1 TABLESPOON: 8 calories, 0 g protein, 2 g carbohydrates, 0 g total fat, 0 g saturated fat, 0 g fiber, 0 mg sodium

CHOCOLATE FROSTING

PREP TIME: 5 MINUTES | **TOTAL TIME:** 5 MINUTES

Makes 1¼ cups

Here's a rich, buttery frosting as good as or better than anything premade. Save a small batch in the refrigerator to put on top of your Coconut-Chocolate Quick Muffin (page 87) for breakfast.

½ cup butter, at room temperature

4 ounces cream cheese, at room temperature

Sweetener equivalent to ½ cup sugar

¼ cup unsweetened cocoa powder

1 tablespoon heavy cream

1 teaspoon vanilla extract

In a medium bowl, with an electric mixer on medium speed, cream the butter, cream cheese, and sweetener until fluffy. Blend in the cocoa, cream, and vanilla and beat until smooth.

PER 1 TABLESPOON: 66 calories, 1 g protein, 1 g carbohydrates, 7 g total fat, 4 g saturated fat, 0 g fiber, 59 mg sodium

VANILLA FROSTING

PREP TIME: 5 MINUTES | **TOTAL TIME:** 5 MINUTES

Makes 1⅓ cups

This quick vanilla frosting works on desserts such as cakes and muffins as well as an Apple-Spice Quick Muffin for breakfast (page 85).

4 ounces butter, at room temperature	1 tablespoon heavy cream
4 ounces cream cheese, at room temperature	1 teaspoon vanilla extract
Sweetener equivalent to ½ cup sugar	

In a medium bowl, with an electric mixer on medium speed, cream the butter, cream cheese, and sweetener until fluffy. Blend in the cream and vanilla and beat until smooth.

PER 1 TABLESPOON: 77 calories, 1 g protein, 1 g carbohydrates, 8 g total fat, 5 g saturated fat, 0 g fiber, 58 mg sodium

COCONUT MACAROONS

PREP TIME: 10 MINUTES | TOTAL TIME: 25 MINUTES

Makes 8 cookies

These simple coconut macaroons require just a few ingredients but will be sure to delight! As with all of the snacks and desserts in this book, because all unhealthy ingredients have been removed and are replaced with healthy substitutes, you can have these macaroons for breakfast as well as for dessert.

To make Orange-Clove-Coconut Macaroons, after adding the sweetener to the egg white mixture, fold in ¼ teaspoon ground cloves, the grated peel of 1 orange, and the juice of half an orange.

3 **egg whites**

¼ **teaspoon cream of tartar**

2 **cups shredded unsweetened coconut**

Sweetener equivalent to ½ cup sugar (see note)

Preheat the oven to 350°F. Line a baking sheet with parchment paper.

In a large bowl, with an electric mixer on high speed, beat the egg whites and cream of tartar until stiff peaks form.

Fold the coconut and sweetener into the egg white mixture.

Scoop the mixture by ¼ cupfuls onto the baking sheet to form 8 mounds. Bake for 15 minutes, or until golden and slightly firm to the touch. Allow to cool before serving.

Note: If using a sweetener with large granules, such as xylitol, grind it in a food processor for 30 seconds, to reduce it to a finer powder, before proceeding with the recipe.

PER COOKIE: 167 calories, 3 g protein, 5 g carbohydrates, 15 g total fat, 13 g saturated fat, 3 g fiber, 27 mg sodium

MOCHA MACAROONS

PREP TIME: 5 MINUTES | **TOTAL TIME:** 20 MINUTES

Makes 20 cookies

Traditional macaroons that have adorned European tables for centuries make a reappearance in our wheat-free lifestyle. These bite-size macaroons can be served alone as a dessert, dipped in whipped cream, topped with Chocolate Glaze (page 214), or served along with custard or ice cream.

2 egg whites

2 cups shredded unsweetened coconut

1 cup All-Purpose Baking Mix (page 19)

Sweetener equivalent to 1 cup sugar

¼ cup + 2 tablespoons unsweetened cocoa powder

2 teaspoons instant coffee granules

¼ teaspoon sea salt

½ cup canned coconut milk

Preheat the oven to 350°F. Line 2 baking sheets with parchment paper.

In a large bowl, with an electric mixer on high speed, beat the egg whites until stiff peaks form.

Fold in the coconut, baking mix, sweetener, cocoa, coffee granules, and salt. Stir in the coconut milk until evenly distributed.

Use a cookie scoop or tablespoon to scoop the mixture into mounds on the baking sheets. Bake for 15 minutes, or until slightly firm to the touch.

PER COOKIE: 113 calories, 3 g protein, 5 g carbohydrates, 10 g total fat, 6 g saturated fat, 3 g fiber, 56 mg sodium

PEANUT BUTTER COOKIES

PREP TIME: 10 MINUTES | **TOTAL TIME:** 25 MINUTES + COOLING TIME

Makes 30

Surely everyone loves peanut butter . . . and everyone loves peanut butter cookies! An especially kid-friendly variation can be made by forming a little depression with a spoon in the center of each cookie prior to baking. When baked and cooled, fill each well with a no-sugar-added fruit spread, such as Plum-Chia Jam (page 51).

Peanut butter can be substituted with any nut or seed butter, such as almond, hazelnut, or sunflower seed.

½ cup All-Purpose Baking Mix (page 19)

½ cup finely chopped peanuts

Sweetener equivalent to ¾ cup sugar

2 cups natural peanut butter, at room temperature

1 tablespoon molasses

2 eggs

1 teaspoon vanilla extract

Preheat the oven to 350°F. Line 2 baking sheets with parchment paper.

In a large bowl, combine the baking mix, nuts, and sweetener. Stir in the peanut butter, molasses, eggs, and vanilla and mix thoroughly.

Use a cookie scoop or tablespoon to scoop the mixture into 1½"-diameter mounds on the baking sheets. Flatten slightly with your hands or with the tines of a fork in a crisscross pattern. Bake for 15 minutes, or until slightly firm and very lightly browned. Cool on the baking sheets for 1 minute. Place on a wire rack to cool completely.

PER COOKIE: 137 calories, 5 g protein, 5 g carbohydrates, 11 g total fat, 1 g saturated fat, 2 g fiber, 78 mg sodium

LEMON-PINEAPPLE SNOWBALLS

PREP TIME: 5 MINUTES | **TOTAL TIME:** 15 MINUTES + CHILLING TIME

Makes 30 snowballs

This may be the fastest way to keep the kids happy in their wheat-free lifestyle: only 15 minutes!

The zesty tropical combination of lemon and pineapple brings these little balls of goodness to life.

2¼ cups shredded unsweetened coconut, divided

1 can (8 ounces) crushed pineapple, drained

Grated peel and juice from 1 lemon

8 ounces cream cheese, at room temperature

Sweetener equivalent to 3 tablespoons sugar

In a food chopper or food processor, briefly pulse 2 cups of the coconut to reduce the size of the coconut shreds. Pour into a large bowl. Place the remaining ¼ cup coconut in a shallow bowl or pie plate and set aside.

To the bowl, add the pineapple, lemon peel and juice, cream cheese, and sweetener. Mix thoroughly.

Use a cookie scoop or tablespoon to scoop the mixture into small mounds onto a plate or baking sheet, and then roll into 1" balls. If the mixture sticks to your hands, moisten them with water. Roll balls in the reserved coconut, return to the plate or baking sheet, and chill for at least 30 minutes before serving.

PER 1 SNOWBALL: 77 calories, 1 g protein, 3 g carbohydrates, 7 g total fat, 5 g saturated fat, 1 g fiber, 26 mg sodium

PECAN-PINEAPPLE BITES

PREP TIME: 15 MINUTES | **TOTAL TIME:** 15 MINUTES + CHILLING TIME

Makes 30 bites

These itsy-bitsy bite-size "bites" are deceptively filling. They are fun and cute enough for the kids, but elegant enough to serve to company.

1 cup ground pecans

3 tablespoons butter, melted

Sweetener equivalent to ¼ cup sugar

1 can (8 ounces) crushed pineapple, drained

8 ounces cream cheese, at room temperature

30 pecan halves

On a baking sheet or large plate, arrange 30 mini paper liners.

In a medium bowl, combine the ground pecans, butter, and sweetener. Mix thoroughly. Spoon evenly into the liners, pressing down with your fingers or a spoon. Set aside.

In another bowl, combine the pineapple and cream cheese. Stir until well blended.

Spoon evenly over the pecan crusts. Place 1 pecan half on top of each. Chill for at least 30 minutes.

PER 1 BITE: 77 calories, 1 g protein, 2 g carbohydrates, 8 g total fat, 2.5 g saturated fat, 1 g fiber, 34 mg sodium

COGNAC TRUFFLES

PREP TIME: 5 MINUTES | **TOTAL TIME:** 30 MINUTES

Makes 30 truffles

Cognac is a deliciously wheat-free and indulgent liquor that mixes perfectly with cocoa. This simple recipe yields a creamy, melt-in-your-mouth treat that lingers with the flavors of your favorite cognac. Serve with espresso at the end of an elegant dinner.

6 ounces unsweetened chocolate, chopped

1 tablespoon molasses

Sweetener equivalent to ½ cup sugar

2 tablespoons cognac

¾ cup heavy cream

¼ cup unsweetened cocoa powder

Line a baking sheet or large plate with parchment paper.

In the top of a double boiler, place the chocolate over simmering water and stir until melted. Stir in the molasses, sweetener, and cognac. Remove from the heat.

Meanwhile, in a large bowl, with an electric mixer on high speed, beat the cream until stiff peaks form. Fold into the chocolate mixture until all the cream is incorporated. The mixture will be relatively stiff.

Place the cocoa powder in a small bowl. Use a tablespoon to scoop out the truffle mixture and, using your hands, form it into balls. Set on the baking sheet or plate. Roll the balls in the cocoa to coat. Chill in an airtight container for up to 1 week.

PER TRUFFLE: 54 calories, 1 g protein, 3 g carbohydrates, 5 g total fat, 3 g saturated fat, 1 g fiber, 4 mg sodium

MACADAMIA NUT FUDGE

PREP TIME: 5 MINUTES | TOTAL TIME: 15 MINUTES + CHILLING TIME

Makes 32 servings

You will be hard-pressed to find anything more indulgent than fudge. Yet here it is in a cookbook designed for health! The macadamias can be replaced with your choice of nuts, such as walnuts, pecans, or pistachios.

8 ounces unsweetened chocolate, chopped

8 ounces cream cheese, at room temperature

Sweetener equivalent to 1 cup sugar

6 tablespoons heavy cream

1 teaspoon vanilla extract

1 teaspoon almond extract

¾ cup unsalted dry-roasted macadamia nuts, chopped

Grease an 8" × 8" baking dish or baking pan.

In the top of a double boiler, place the chocolate over simmering water and stir until melted. Alternately, place the chocolate in a microwaveable bowl and microwave on high power in 15-second increments, stirring in between, until smooth.

Meanwhile, in a medium bowl, with an electric mixer on medium speed, beat the cream cheese and sweetener until creamy. Add the cream, vanilla, and almond extract and mix to combine. Stir in the chocolate until well combined. Stir in the nuts. Spread into the baking dish or baking pan and chill until firm.

PER SERVING: 92 calories, 2 g protein, 3 g carbohydrates, 10 g total fat, 5 g saturated fat, 1 g fiber, 24 mg sodium

DARK CHOCOLATE–NUT CRUNCH

PREP TIME: 5 MINUTES | **TOTAL TIME:** 10 MINUTES + CHILLING TIME

Makes 15 servings

This rich treat is great as is or spread with a bit of almond butter.

8 ounces dark chocolate (85% cocoa), chopped

1 teaspoon coconut oil

2 cups mixed raw or dry-roasted nuts (such as pistachios, cashews, almonds, Brazil nuts, walnuts, pecans, and macadamia nuts), roughly chopped

Line a 9" x 9" baking dish with parchment paper or foil.

In the top of a double boiler, place the chocolate and oil over simmering water and stir until smooth. Remove from the heat. Add the nuts, stirring to coat with the chocolate.

Spread the mixture evenly into the baking dish. Refrigerate for 30 minutes, or until set. Break into pieces.

PER SERVING: 170 calories, 5 g protein, 8 g carbohydrates, 16 g total fat, 6 g saturated fat, 4 g fiber, 87 mg sodium

SPICY MIXED NUTS

PREP TIME: 5 MINUTES | **TOTAL TIME:** 15 MINUTES

Makes 4 cups

Mixed nuts purchased at the store are invariably coated with hydrogenated ("trans") fats to allow the salt to stick to the nuts. This converts something wonderful for health—nuts—into something awful for health due to the trans fats. Tasty dry-roasted nuts without the nastiness of trans fats can be re-created very easily.

For simplicity and time, I put the seasoning mixes to work. However, if desired, they are easily substituted with your choice of seasonings, such as garlic powder, onion powder, paprika, crushed pepper, and salt.

4 **cups raw nuts (such as almonds, walnuts, pecans, pistachios, Brazil nuts, and hazelnuts; also consider raw pumpkin seeds or sunflower seeds)**

2 **tablespoons coconut oil, melted**

1–2 **tablespoons Cajun Seasoning Mix (page 58) or Taco Seasoning Mix (page 57)**

½ **teaspoon sea salt**

Preheat the oven to 350°F.

In a large bowl, combine the nuts, oil, seasoning mix, and salt. Toss until well mixed.

Spread on a shallow baking pan and bake for 10 minutes, stirring once, or until lightly toasted and fragrant.

PER ¼ CUP: 193 calories, 5 g protein, 6 g carbohydrates, 18 g total fat, 3 g saturated fat, 3 g fiber, 61 mg sodium

CHIPOTLE PEPPER ROASTED ALMONDS

PREP TIME: 5 MINUTES | **TOTAL TIME:** 25 MINUTES

Makes 2 cups

Here's a nut mix for anyone who really loves spicy seasonings with the flavors of chipotle pepper, ground red pepper, and horseradish.

- 2 cups raw almonds
- 1 teaspoon ground chipotle chile pepper
- 1 teaspoon chili powder
- ½ teaspoon ground red pepper (optional)
- 1 teaspoon horseradish powder
- 1 teaspoon mustard powder
- 2 teaspoons sea salt
- 2 teaspoons coconut oil, melted
- 2 teaspoons vinegar

Preheat the oven to 275°F.

In a medium bowl, combine the almonds, chipotle pepper, chili powder, red pepper, horseradish, mustard, salt, and oil. Mix thoroughly. Stir in the vinegar.

Spread on a shallow baking pan and bake for 20 minutes, stirring once, or until lightly toasted and fragrant.

PER ¼ CUP: 225 calories, 8 g protein, 8 g carbohydrates, 19 g total fat, 2 g saturated fat, 5 g fiber, 394 mg sodium

HORSERADISH–SOY SAUCE ROASTED ALMONDS

PREP TIME: 5 MINUTES | **TOTAL TIME:** 25 MINUTES

Makes 8 servings (2 cups)

This is one homemade variation on those spicy, flavored canned almonds you can buy at the store. When you make them yourself, they come with no wheat, maltodextrin, textured vegetable protein, and all the other stuff that you and I don't add.

- 2 cups raw almonds
- 1 teaspoon horseradish powder
- 1 teaspoon mustard powder
- 2 teaspoons sea salt
- 2 teaspoons gluten-free tamari or soy sauce
- 2 teaspoons coconut oil, melted
- 2 teaspoons vinegar

Preheat the oven to 275°F.

In a medium bowl, combine the almonds, horseradish, mustard, salt, tamari or soy sauce, and oil. Mix thoroughly. Stir in the vinegar.

Spread on a shallow baking pan and bake for 20 minutes, stirring once, or until lightly toasted and fragrant.

PER SERVING (¼ CUP): 219 calories, 8 g protein, 8 g carbohydrates, 19 g total fat, 2 g saturated fat, 5 g fiber, 472 mg sodium

CHOCOLATE PEANUT BUTTER CAKE

PREP TIME: 5 MINUTES | **TOTAL TIME:** 5 MINUTES

Makes 1 serving

Missing a candy treat? This quick mini cake will satisfy any sweet tooth.

3 tablespoons almond flour/meal

1 tablespoon ground golden flaxseeds

2 tablespoons unsweetened cocoa powder

Sweetener equivalent to 2 tablespoons sugar

¼ teaspoon baking powder

¼ salt

1 tablespoon peanut butter, softened

2 tablespoons milk

1 tablespoon coconut oil or melted butter

In a coffee mug with a fork, stir together the almond meal, flaxseeds, cocoa powder, sweetener, baking powder, and salt until smooth. Mix together the peanut butter, milk, and oil or butter. Mix into the dry ingredients and microwave on high for 1 to 2 minutes until set. Eat with a dollop of Greek yogurt or whipped cream.

PER SERVING: 313 calories, 9 g protein, 15 g carbohydrates, 29 g total fat, 14 g saturated fat, 8 g fiber, 423 mg sodium

MENUS FOR
SPECIAL OCCASIONS

HERE ARE THEMED menus to suit a number of special occasions, from Sunday Brunch to Pub Night to Chinese Takeout. Of course, you can follow any of these menus even when it's not a special occasion, when you're just in the mood for an interesting meal!

Entire menus cannot, of course, be assembled in a 30-minute timeline, so plan accordingly. All menu items can be made from recipes in this cookbook except those marked with an asterisk (*).

FRIDAY NIGHT PIZZA

It's all about the pizza and the company you keep with Friday Night Pizza! There are endless variations on the combinations of meats, vegetables, and cheeses for pizza; the two recipes provided in this cookbook are unique starting places. Since beer is a popular accompaniment to pizza, several safe beers are listed, too.

- Provolone, Prosciutto, and Kalamata Olive Pizza (page 155) or Kale, Onion, and Goat Cheese Pizza (page 185)

- Apple Pie Whoopies (page 204) or Cinnamon Roll Whoopies (page 205) or Plum Jam Whoopies (page 206)

- Gluten-free beer (such as Bard's, Green's, Redbridge) or wheat-free but not gluten-free beer for the non-celiac or non-gluten-sensitive (such as Michelob Ultra or Bud Light)

TEX-MEX NIGHT

Have some fresh salsa or pico de gallo on hand for a fun and spicy Mexican Night!

- Guacamole (page 32) and Pita Chips (page 27)

- Barbecue Beef Quesadillas (page 140)

- Poblano Pepper and Beef Tortillas (page 145) or Chorizo-Shrimp Tortillas (page 179)

- Taco Lettuce Wraps (page 144)

- Vanilla Custard (page 211) topped with crushed pecans, Chocolate Glaze (page 214), and cinnamon

PUB NIGHT

Get your family together for an evening of fun foods. Good news: Although the menu sounds like a list of junk foods, none are junk!

These recipes transform ordinarily indulgent foods with unhealthy ingredients into healthy dishes with no downside. Enjoy your meal and don't be concerned about weight gain, heartburn, or any of those nasty wheat-related worries!

- Spicy Mixed Nuts (page 227) or Chipotle Pepper Roasted Almonds (page 228)

- Barbecue Bacon-Wrapped Chicken (page 161)

- Spicy Chicken Thighs (page 157)

- Pepperoni Bread (page 108)

- Peanut Butter Cookies (page 221)

- Gluten-free beer (such as Bard's, Green's, Redbridge) or wheat-free but not gluten-free beer for the non-celiac or non-gluten-sensitive (such as Michelob Ultra or Bud Light)

CHINESE TAKEOUT

You won't be hungry in 2 hours after this Chinese meal! Be sure to have some gluten-free soy sauce or tamari, as well as some hot mustard sauce, on hand, if desired.

- Brewed green tea*

- Egg Drop Soup (page 95)

- Japanese Eggplant Stir-Fry over shirataki noodles (page 190)

- Pork Fried "Rice" (page 133)

- Vanilla Custard (page 211) sprinkled with freshly ground or dried nutmeg or Pistachio–Green Tea Cupcakes (page 200)

SUMMER PICNIC

A refreshing salad, a light sandwich or wrap, cupcakes, sunlight . . . with no after-meal heartburn, sleepiness, or weight gain: Does life get any better than that?

- Cucumber, red onion, and tomato salad* with Dilled Cucumber Yogurt Sauce (page 38)

- Avocado-Ham Sandwiches (page 105) or Tex-Mex Egg Salad Wraps (page 113) or Pepperoni Pizza Wraps (page 116)

- Tart Tangerine Cupcakes (page 201)

ROMANTIC EVENING

Romantic dinners mean foods with subtle and fragrant nuances, not overly elaborate but prepared with care, ending with something lightly indulgent.

Wine and digestive suggestions are included for those so inclined.

- Moroccan Chicken with Roasted Bell Peppers (page 156) or Parmesan-Crusted Cod (page 169) or Steak Béarnaise (page 136)

- Wines with dinner: Pinot Grigio with chicken or cod; Merlot or Cabernet Sauvignon with steak

- Artichokes, Pancetta, and Kale with Shaved Parmesan (page 121) or Crab-Stuffed Portobellos (page 127) or Italian Marinated Mushrooms (page 126)

- Tomato and Fennel Soup (page 94) or green salad with Moroccan Dressing (page 48)

- Cognac Truffles (page 224) or Double Chocolate Mini Cakes (page 198) or Coconut Macaroons (page 219)

- Courvoisier or other Cognac

MOVIE NIGHT

Here are finger foods to munch with your drama, love story, or comedy!

- Spicy Mixed Nuts (page 227) or Horseradish–Soy Sauce Roasted Almonds (page 229)

- Dark Chocolate–Nut Crunch (page 226)

- Ice Cream Sandwiches (Vanilla Custard, page 211, sandwiched between two Peanut Butter Cookies, page 221) or Cinnamon Doughnuts (page 196)

ITALIAN NIGHT

Minus the Italian bread and wheat-based pasta, you can still have a wonderful and varied Italian-style meal that relies on the flavors of tomato, oregano, basil, portobello mushrooms, and red wine.

- Green salad with halved fresh mozzarella balls and cherry tomatoes*, topped with Spicy Italian Dressing (page 49)

- Italian Sausage Meatballs with Red Wine Sauce (page 109) served over shirataki fettuccine

- Italian Marinated Mushrooms (page 126) or Crab-Stuffed Portobellos (page 127)

- Breakfast Cheesecake (page 74) with Strawberry Glaze (page 216)

NEW ORLEANS JAMBOREE

You don't need to wait for Fat Tuesday to enjoy the wonderful flavors of New Orleans! Finish this spicy dinner menu with the smooth coolness of vanilla custard topped with caramel, accompanied by a rich café au lait.

- Deviled eggs made with Spicy Cajun Mayo (page 42)

- Jambalaya (page 152) or Cajun Baked Fish with Shrimp Cream Sauce (page 168) or Cajun Chicken Cutlets (page 162)

- Cajun Kale (page 124)

- Vanilla Custard (page 211) with pecans and Caramel Sauce (page 212)

- Café au lait*

INDIAN NIGHT

For an adventurous night of exotic foods, try this mix of flavorful Indian dishes, topped off with a burst of citrusy Lemon-Pineapple Snowballs and the heady flavors of chai tea.

If you are making more than one curried dish, consider distinguishing them by choosing different varieties of curry for each, such as vindaloo curry for the shrimp and a garam masala mixture for the rice or vegetables.

• Curried "Rice" (page 132) or Curried Vegetables (page 183)

• Indian Curry Shrimp (page 180)

• Palak Paneer (page 186)

• Lemon-Pineapple Snowballs (page 222)

• Chai tea with coconut milk*

SUNDAY BRUNCH

This one will take some work! This is the sort of spread you might anticipate for a big family get-together. One interesting observation you may make: Your guests will eat less than they would at a conventional Sunday brunch because your brunch contains no appetite stimulants. They can relish your wonderful cooking without worrying about gaining weight and—especially important for anyone with diabetes—without experiencing any substantial rise in blood sugar. You and your guests can just eat and enjoy it!

- Lox Wraps (page 117)

- Wasabi Deviled Eggs (page 103)

- Cream of Mushroom Soup with Chives (page 92)

- Italian Sausage Meatballs with Red Wine Sauce (page 109)

- Crab-Stuffed Portobellos (page 127) or Italian Marinated Mushrooms (page 126)

- Fillet of Fish Amandine (page 170)

- Chicken Piccata (page 163) or Barbecue Bacon-Wrapped Chicken (page 161)

- Roasted Zucchini, Squash, and Tomato Medley (page 131)

- Apple Streusel Muffins (page 203) or Key Lime Cupcakes (page 199) or Pistachio–Green Tea Cupcakes (page 200) or Tart Tangerine Cupcakes (page 201) or Macadamia-Spice Muffins (page 202)

- Optional: dry (brut or extra brut) champagne, sparkling wine, or prosecco

WINTER LUNCH

If you live in a colder climate like I do, you know how wonderful a hot lunch with familiar comfort foods can be on a cold winter day. Most conventional notions of comfort food, however, mean plenty of blood sugar problems and weight gain. As with all of my recipes, these comfort foods can be eaten . . . well, comfortably, without those sorts of worries!

- New England Clam Chowder (page 99) or Cream of Mushroom Soup with Chives (page 92)

- Balsamic Mushroom Wraps (page 115) or Tex-Mex Egg Salad Wraps (page 113)

- Berry-Coconut Mini Cheesecakes (page 195)

BACKYARD BARBECUE

Eating outdoors is one of the truly simple pleasures in life. In this menu, simplicity is the theme, allowing you to enjoy the sun and outdoors more with less cooking fuss. To simplify preparation, make the Pita Chips ahead of time or keep a supply on hand. Sun tea can likewise be made earlier in the day.

• Guacamole (page 32) and Pita Chips (page 27)

• Pork ribs* brushed with Barbecue Sauce (page 35)

• Grilled fresh asparagus or other vegetables*

• Coconut-Chocolate Tart (page 194)

• Iced tea or sun tea with mint leaves*

APPENDIX
Wheat-Free Resources

THERE ARE PLENTY of resources available for people with celiac disease or gluten sensitivity. They are primarily useful to help identify hidden sources of gluten, locate restaurants and stores that sell gluten-free foods, and find physicians familiar with the special needs of people who have celiac disease.

Because *Wheat Belly* and the *Wheat Belly Cookbook* introduce the idea that wheat elimination is not just for people with celiac disease or gluten sensitivity, but for everyone, the resources that target this larger audience are still limited, though they will likely grow rapidly as this concept catches on.

In the meantime, some resources for products, additional wheat-free recipes, and more information are listed on the following pages. Resources for those who have celiac disease or gluten sensitivity are included as well.

Nuts, Seeds, Nut Meals, and Flours

Sources for nuts, seeds, nut meals, and flours may be as close as your supermarket. However, it really pays to shop around, as prices vary widely (as much as sixfold—600 percent!). The most economical method is usually to grind nut meals and flours yourself in a food chopper, food processor, or coffee grinder. However, most major supermarkets and health food stores carry preground nut meals and flours. Seed meals are rarely sold preground but are very easy to grind from whole sesame, sunflower, chia, or pumpkin seeds.

Bob's Red Mill is a nationally distributed brand and an excellent source of high-quality (often organic) almond flour, coconut flour, garbanzo bean (chickpea) flour, and xanthan gum.

Trader Joe's is a very affordable source for nearly all the whole nuts and seeds you need. They also have ground almond meal for a great price. Whole Foods Market is another, though high-cost, source for most nuts, seeds, meals, and flours.

The online retailers below have extensive choices of nuts, seeds, and nut and seed flours and meals, including almond meal, almond flour, and chia.

www.nuts.com
www.ohnuts.com
www.nutstop.com
www.diamondnuts.com
www.nutsonthenet.com
www.nutiva.com

Sweeteners

Start with your local grocery store or health food store for liquid stevia, powdered stevia (pure stevia or made with inulin), or Truvía. Health food stores, in particular, typically have several choices of stevia, since it has been available for several years as a nutritional supplement.

Erythritol and xylitol are not always available in grocery stores. Check health food stores, but you may need to order online. Nuts.com carries xylitol, and Amazon carries several brands of xylitol and erythritol, including NOW, KAL, and Emerald Forest.

You can also find erythritol and xylitol at:

www.wheatfreemarket.com
www.luckyvitamin.com
www.4allvitamins.com
www.iherb.com

Monk Fruit (Luo han guo):

www.wheatfreemarket.com
www.intheraw.com

Shirataki Noodles

Bigger and better-stocked grocery stores will often carry shirataki noodles, though look for them in the refrigerated section, not on the pasta shelf. If not available in your grocery store, these noodles can be purchased online. Miracle and House Foods are two good brands.

Celiac Disease Resources

Here are additional resources for individuals with celiac disease or gluten sensitivity. They are useful for helping identify foods containing gluten, and some of these organizations maintain lists of restaurants that accommodate safe gluten-free eating. The Gluten Intolerance Group, for instance, maintains a list of gluten-free restaurants searchable by state or zip code. The Celiac Disease Foundation's Web site also provides links to the Web sites of the various gluten-free food manufacturers. The Celiac Sprue Association provides a wealth of resources, including a phone-in hotline for members ($50 for a 2-year membership).

These organizations also provide support to restaurants and food manufacturers needing guidance on creating a gluten-free food preparation environment. The National Foundation for Celiac Awareness, for instance, offers a food service training program.

These organizations are supported by donations and product sales. However, buyer beware: Much of the revenue that supports these organizations comes from manufacturers of gluten-free foods. It means that they tend to steer you toward these products, which are best avoided entirely. Nonetheless, these organizations can serve as a useful starting place for more information relevant to celiac disease and gluten sensitivity.

CeliacCorner
www.celiaccorner.com

Celiac Disease Foundation
www.celiac.org

Celiac Sprue Association
www.csaceliacs.info

Gluten Intolerance Group
www.gluten.net

National Foundation for Celiac Awareness
www.celiaccentral.org

Gluten-Free Prescription Drugs and Nutritional Supplements

Steve Plogsted, PharmD, runs a Web site (www.glutenfreedrugs.com) that serves as a good starting place to investigate the gluten content of prescription drugs.

With nutritional supplements, always check the label. Nutritional supplements are often labeled "gluten-free," as well as listing the absence of other potential undesirable components, such as lactose.

Additional Recipes

Cookbooks in the low-carbohydrate and "paleo" diets overlap to a great extent with the sorts of foods advocated in this cookbook. Their recipes are wheat-free and focus on real food ingredients.

Just be careful: Some of the recipes in these cookbooks tend to use unhealthy sweeteners—such as maple syrup, honey, and agave—or occasionally rely too heavily on "safe" starches like sweet potatoes or yams and rice. These carbohydrate sources are indeed safer than wheat and sugar, but they are not entirely healthy when consumed in larger quantities, such as more than a ½-cup serving.

Likewise, be careful with gluten-free cookbooks, as they often use unhealthy gluten-free replacements, such as rice starch/flour, cornstarch, potato starch, tapioca starch, or premixed gluten-free flours. My advice: Never use these starches. Avoid the recipes that call for them, and select only the ones that do not use these gluten-free flours.

Web Sites

Stay-at-home mom turned wheat/gluten-free, low-carb recipe writer Carolyn Ketchum provides great recipes accompanied by excellent photography.
www.alldayidreamaboutfood.com

Elana Amsterdam's beautiful and creative mostly almond flour–based recipes are featured on her Web site/blog, as well as in her cookbook listed in the next section.
www.elanaspantry.com

Formally trained in culinary arts, blogger Michelle provides great recipes that are free of wheat/gluten and corn.
www.glutenfreefix.com

Nutritionist Maria Emmerich is a wheat-free, limited-carbohydrate champion! She is among the few nutritionists who truly understand these important health concepts. The photography on her Web site is also stunningly beautiful. Maria's excellent cookbook is listed below.
www.mariahealth.blogspot.com

Books

The Art of Healthy Eating: Kids and *The Art of Healthy Eating: Sweets* by Maria Emmerich (CreateSpace, 2011)

Eat Like a Dinosaur: Recipe and Guidebook for Gluten-Free Kids by The Paleo Parents (Victory Belt Publishing, 2012)

Everyday Paleo by Sarah Fragoso (Victory Belt Publishing, 2011)

500 Paleo Recipes by Dana Carpender (Fair Winds Press, 2012)

The G-Free Diet: A Gluten-Free Survival Guide by Elisabeth Hasselbeck (Center Street, 2011)

Gather: The Art of Paleo Entertaining by Hayley Mason and Bill Staley (Victory Belt Publishing, 2013)

The Gluten-Free Almond Flour Cookbook by Elana Amsterdam (Celestial Arts, 2009)

The Gluten-Free Asian Kitchen by Laura B. Russell (Celestial Arts, 2011)

The Gluten-Free Bible: The Thoroughly Indispensable Guide to Negotiating Life without Wheat by Jax Peters Lowell (Holt Paperbacks, 2005)

The Gluten-Free Edge: Get Skinny the Gluten-Free Way! by Gini Warner and Chef Ross Harris (Adams Media, 2011)

Grain-Free Gourmet by Jodi Bager and Jenny Lass (Whitecap Books Ltd., 2010)

The Healthy Gluten-Free Life by Tammy Credicott (Victory Belt Publishing, 2012)

Make It Paleo by Bill Staley and Hayley Mason (Victory Belt Publishing, 2011)

Nutritious and Delicious by Maria Emmerich (Self, 2012)

1001 Low-Carb Recipes by Dana Carpender (Fair Winds Press, 2010)

Paleo Comfort Foods by Julie and Charles Mayfield (Victory Belt Publishing, 2011)

Paleo Cooking from Elana's Pantry by Elana Amsterdam (Ten Speed Press, 2013)

The Paleo Diet and *The Paleo Diet Cookbook* by Loren Cordain (Houghton Mifflin Harcourt 2010)

Practical Paleo by Diane Sanfilippo (Victory Belt Publishing, 2012)

The Primal Blueprint Cookbook by Mark Sisson and Jennifer Meier (Primal Nutrition, 2010)

More *Wheat Belly* Resources

Wheat Belly (Rodale, 2011)

This is the original book, released in August 2011, that details all the reasons why humans have no business eating modern wheat.

The Wheat Belly Blog, Facebook page, and YouTube videos provide ongoing discussions about many issues relevant to wheat and living wheat free, as well as real stories of people who have discovered this lifestyle. I also post new recipes here.

Many articles, podcasts, and TV interviews are archived on the blog.
www.wheatbellyblog.com
www.facebook.com/pages/Wheat-Belly
www.youtube.com/user/wheatbelly

Wheat-Free Research and Education Foundation

This is the organization I've helped establish that will, in the future, fund research, provide education, and help inform the public about the need to recognize the dangers of wheat consumption and the health benefits of ridding your life of it.
www.wheatfreeref.org

INDEX

Underscored page references indicate boxed text. An asterisk(*) indicates that photographs appear in the color insert pages.